CHANGE YOUR CLOTHES

TERRI DAVIS

Copyright © 2016 by Terri Davis.

Library of Congress Control Number:		2016905940
ISBN:	Hardcover	978-1-5144-8352-7
	Softcover	978-1-5144-8351-0
	eBook	978-1-5144-8350-3

All rights reserved. No part of this book may be reproduced or transmitted in any form or by any means, electronic or mechanical, including photocopying, recording, or by any information storage and retrieval system, without permission in writing from the copyright owner.

Scripture quotations marked KJV are from the Holy Bible, King James Version (Authorized Version). First published in 1611. Quoted from the KJV Classic Reference Bible, Copyright © 1983 by The Zondervan Corporation.

Any people depicted in stock imagery provided by Thinkstock are models, and such images are being used for illustrative purposes only. Certain stock imagery © Thinkstock.

Print information available on the last page.

Rev. date: 04/13/2016

To order additional copies of this book, contact:
Xlibris
1-888-795-4274
www.Xlibris.com
Orders@Xlibris.com
739379

Table of Contents

Foreword vii
Dedication xi
Introduction xiii
1. Change your Clothes 1
2. Pursue and Overtake 4
3. The Sound of Abundant Rain 7
4. Much too Good! 9
5. How Did I Get Here? 13
6. Seek Ye First 16
7. What Are You Waiting For? 18
8. It is Your Season 22
9. Be Made Whole 24
10. Daddy 28
11. Remember this White Boy 31
12. Catching Up with Me 34
13. Girl, Don't You Know Your Worth? 36
14. My Body Belongs to God 40
15. Spirit of Gluttony 43
16. I Forgot About Sorrow 45
17. Let the Truth Be Told 49
18. So Traditional 52
19. The Struggle that Has Been 54
20. Two 'Sistas' and a French Fry 58
21. We Will Make it 61
22. Strengthen Me 64
23. I Need a Word from You 66
24. Down in the Dumps:
    Whom to Blame? 68
25. Where My Help Comes From 74
26. The Lord 78
27. He Will Use 80
28. Mighty 83
29. What I Treasure Most 86
30. If You Love Me 89

31. Am I Really Trying?	92
32. Be Glad in it	94
33. Time Waits for No One	96
34. Birth, Pregnancy, Conception	99
35. Thank you, Lord!	103
36. A Masterpiece in the Making	105
37. My Love Letter to God	107
Closing	109
Terri Davis	111

Foreword

So often today, we applaud someone's *transparency* in communicating with others. Too often, we do so without fully understanding the *gift* that is being shared; to be "transparent" is to be "free from guile; candid or open" (American Heritage Dictionary). Let us always give thanks to our heavenly Father Who strategically positions His child as a prism of *light* in a world full of "darkness." Such a light then becomes a reflection of Jesus, of God's abundant love and grace. Every life experience —good and bad —serves as an opportunity to showcase the enormity of God's *amazing grace* when His children bow and bend in humble recognition and gratitude of His will and way —when we recognize that God lavishes ours lives with love, and every journey is a gift.

Terri Davis's faith journey calls each reader to **Change Your Clothes.** Her compilation of profound, poignant selections of poetry and testimony shares with us her immense sensitivity, breakthroughs, relevance and reality, failures and victory. Terri's message — ordained for this season —results from her *conception* of truth [relationship with Jesus] as a young teen seeking identity, to her *birth* as a woman full of faith. What a divine set-up! One cannot help but be thrust into every poetic utterance and accompanying word of encouragement with a sense of awe and gratitude to God for this timely gift, enfolded by His Holy Spirit.

If having overcome enormous trials by the "blood of the Lamb and the word of her testimony" helps to change just one wrongful path, then Terri has accomplished her purpose. If "No holding back!" causes just one soul to repent of sin and walk in the Light of Jesus, then this is the true measure of witnessing. If being transparent is to "put off garments of sorrow for those of praise," then Terri selflessly "changed her clothes" — more importantly, her life and that of others!

Terri's poems are penned with carefully chosen words of truth and relevance to one's 'inner man'— reaching deep into recesses of soul and spirit. She also explains clearly the road taken (or not), through real and practical illustrations, and portrays vividly the constant care of a loving God.

Certainly, the same Father who kept His daughter along the way even when she could not "see" her way will do the same for you and me. Therefore, the overarching gift of this marvelous work is not so much the author's own *transparency* as it is that "open door" to every reader to unwrap God's gift: Wherever you may be on life's journey, it's never too late to receive and acknowledge God's ***unconditional love*** —love found only through Jesus the Christ. Such acceptance is true transparency, for when all is said and done, **Jesus** alone is the **Light** shining through!

Elder Ada White Taylor, D.Min.

Change Your Life

But there's also this, it's not too late —
GOD's personal Message! —
"Come back to me and really mean it!
Come fasting and weeping, sorry for your sins!"

Change your life, not just your clothes.
Come back to GOD, *your* God.
And here's why: God is kind and merciful.
He takes a deep breath, puts up with a lot,
This most patient God, extravagant in love,
always ready to cancel catastrophe.
Who knows? Maybe he'll do it now,
maybe he'll turn around and show pity.
Maybe, when all's said and done,
there'll be blessings full and robust for your God!

(Joel 2:12-14 AMP).

Dedication

This Book is dedicated to the loving memory of my sister Natalie Rae Evans.

To my Loving Sister Latoria Evans, and my brother in his absence, my sweet mother Joyce Evans Whitaker, and to my children, Diedra, Isiah, Tierra, and my nephew Tony- how can I say "Thank you" for loving me through it all and always being there for your mother— I love you so much.

To all of my nieces and nephews: Jamiah, Sycorey, Destiny, Shamik, and Finesse, son-in-laws Broderick, Anthony, and my sweet Alyssa— I love you.

Andre& Marshelle Williams, Deborah & Wayne Thomas, Dana Devine, Roysanne & Carla Satterfield, Debra & Vickie Hubby, To all of my Elders: Elder Bernard Williams, Carla Stokes, Elder Craig Heath, Elder Vanetta West, Elder Ada Taylor, thank you. To New Birth praise team, I love and miss you. To my loving Bishop, I love you. To pastor's Matthew & Sabrina, and Grace praise team, thank you, and everyone who stood by me to help me stand, thank you. Much love! Synthe M. Fleming you are a phenomenon, and I love you girl.

Introduction

I was inspired to write about several events that occurred through my transition of change. Changing hasn't always come easily; in fact the more I think about it, I was not even considering changing my way of living until God stepped into my life and began ministering to me. My whole world turned in a different and unfamiliar direction. I was afraid and on many occasions paralyzed by the fear of moving from my familiar way of life. I was sometimes disobedient, for when God wanted me to go one way I would go the other. I had to repent! The moment I allowed change was the moment I began my journey to destiny.

Change is very common in the world we live in. With technology, markets up and down, our children growing up (They are not infants anymore, and neither are we!), it is evident that we *experience* change but the question is will we *accept* it in our hearts. I can say that with God it will be a more pleasant transition. Change is going to come whether we are ready for it or not; so I encourage you to embrace change as it comes. It may not be easy but it is always good. It may be joyous for some, and so unexpected for others that many may change kicking and screaming. Whether you are the kicker or screamer, remember to repent. The key is to change.

God told Jacob to gather his people and go up to Bethel to worship, and to put away their idols (see Genesis 35:2-5). God is calling us to do the same. He wants us to experience everything that He created us for —which will only come with our changing. As you walk with me through these pages, I hope that you will not just laugh but think about how important it is for your future that you do change. Most of all, I pray that you will connect with this writing and use it as a tool to move forward. These testimonies are from my heart to yours in hope that you will see there are so many in this world going through similar changes, and to assure you that you are not alone.

Never did I think the day would come when I would be sharing a part of my life with an audience or be fortunate enough to share my testimonies with you. Well, this day has come and it came because I became hungry for change. I hope that as you read, you will discover your potential to change and do so NOW.

May our God richly bless you!
Terri Davis

Change your Clothes

Take off your old and put on the new
Stand up . . . we are forgiven
Be courageous and bold, God is calling you
To wake up and get back to living
We are finished with the struggles and strife
We stir up our gifts to leave legacy in life
Standing up in our faith as we are walking in kingdom
We take back our right, our belief and our freedom
Embracing opportunity that we have been given
Here to take over, but most of all to live in
Our time and our season, and as a matter of fact
We have changed our clothes and we take our life back.

(Genesis 35:2-5)

Change Your Clothes

Has there ever been a time that you just knew you had messed up? I mean you messed up bad! —so badly that you kept looking above to make sure God was not going to reach down and snatch you up. To top it off, it seemed that everyone else knew that you messed up, too. Hello! I can testify to that . . . my stuff was flapping in the wind like a flag on a flagpole. I knew how well deserved the repercussions of that sin were . . . amazing part about it all was God knew it, too, but He still forgave! The true blessing was that He did not hold it against me.

Today you may be reflecting on a moment like that or maybe something similar. You may even be taking a deep breath right now thinking about that moment, because you knew it was your end. That day you called on God with a fervent heart, puffy eyes, and your nose red from crying out to Him, possibly all night. Then all of a sudden, here comes what I call "the twins"—Grace and Mercy. At that very moment of redemption, you felt the wind from the gates of hell —you were now uninvited to their party because of the blood of Jesus Christ. Guess what! The Lord forgave you and He still forgives. Thank You, Lord!

Sometimes our challenge is getting out of the 'familiar.' Familiar has held so many captive for such a long time, and I do mean many years. The challenge is to not stay in that mess that has brought so much unhappiness, so much pain. Many folks (not you, but your neighbor) would rather live like this than move out on faith. Yes, I admit that I have been there, too. But God! God's desire is to move us from that place. God wants to see us flourish like a beautiful flower in its season. He knows that there will be bumps along the way; that is why Jesus came, to assure us that we could make it past all of the bumps in life (which, by the way, are distractions). God does not want us to go back down that old, familiar path or make that same wrong choice again.

I know that most of you reading this might say, "It is easier said than done." Well, let us think about God's feelings: He has sent and sacrificed His only child to keep us from harm; yet most people have decided to stay in harm's way, believing it is better than moving into something they do not know about. Imagine someone saying to you, "I see your station wagon has given you a hard time and so I did something special for you: Here are keys to your new car—a Mercedes. It's yours!" You then turn around (with your 'intelligent self') and reply, "No, thanks! This car has been in our family for years; it always has this problem, and I can't see parting with it, but thank you anyway." Think how hurt and disappointed the giver would be with such a response. Their only hope and desire was to see that you had 'better' . . . and you missed the whole point —the great blessing of your life —because you wanted to stay in your familiar. Do you get my drift?

This has happened more often than we would want to admit, allowing distractions to keep us from moving ahead. Please, stop it! In Genesis 35:2-5 God told Jacob to arise and go up to Bethel (please read the passage for yourself). He said, "Go up . . .," meaning to move forward not backward; not to stand still but to get up and out of those familiar surroundings. Let go of the idols, the man, the woman or any personal agendas that have held you captive. Stop being paralyzed by what you see or hear; move out on what God is showing you!

God directed them to make an altar there. When you have been delivered, remember to never forget the One who brought you out —worship Him! Keep Him first. When God is your priority, your life will be at its best, come storm or rain, for He will hide you. When our ways please God, He gives us peace not only with Himself but also with man. There are so many benefits in God; give Him the chance to show you.

Changing the way we do things will make a world of difference for our present and our future. Think about the children: Do we want them to keep making the same decisions to do wrong after we have invested so much love into seeing them be their best? Of course not! Well, this is how God, our heavenly Father, feels about you and me. Now get up and get back to living!

Pursue and Overtake

We know what to do
And we will not sit back
Pursue, overtake
Go out and attack

The weapons of our warfare
Are not carnal at all
They pull down strongholds
And break through walls

Taking back the peace
That is ours to keep
Promising His loved ones
The sweetest of sleep

Overtake and pursue
Because we leap over walls
Running through troops
And recovering all

Take back all the rights
That were hidden in sin
Captured and enslaved
Imprisoned within

Pursue and conquer all!

(I Samuel 30: 8)

Testimony of Encouragement
(Pursue and Overtake)

Oh my goodness, I could have run all over the church in service today! —Bishop "preached his socks off!" Not only did he talk about David from I Samuel chapter 30, verse 8, he called us to the altar to receive a double dose of the anointing flowing over him and then prophetically spoke into many lives. I wanted to go up and throw my handkerchief at him (smile) —it was just that good!

Well, here is my point: I was so encouraged I came home to continue writing this book. That was this morning and now here it is almost midnight; it has been hard for me to get away from this laptop. I have been back and forth, with what I should do or need to do in this life in order to leave a blessing for my children and their children —something that really weighed heavily upon me. Now here I am writing a book! Who knew?

The Bible says, *"A good man leaves an inheritance for his children, and their children"* (see Proverbs 13:22). I had thought it [my legacy] would be my music and that it would have happened already, but it has not *yet!* I am not sure where or when it will come but I do know that it will. I will keep walking by faith and doing what the Spirit has put in my heart to do. I hope that someone grabs that little "golden nugget" (*Lol*).

Maybe you are unsure of what direction you need to go: Take a moment to stop and pray; talk to the Father. He is listening and He will always come through. Once you have prayed begin to walk out what He puts in your heart to do. Proverbs 3:5-6 tells us how to walk it out: *"Trust in the LORD with all your heart and lean not on your own understanding; in all your ways acknowledge him, and he will make your paths straight."*

Maybe like me, you kept coming back to what you love the most . . . as a matter of fact, you know what you were created for— your *love*. Well, this is my sincerest advice: Offer it up to God. I know that may sound a little challenging for most but I have found that it is *the* better way; and it will "come to pass," because God is the Author and Finisher . . . .

Every new day I find other things occupy my attention and keep me away from my music ministry. Am I still working at it? Yes, I am. I still have the passion for it and I believe the promises of God that I will minister all over this world, singing to His glory! We as saints must be discerning folks, knowing there is a time and season for everything.

In every season, make sure that you are bringing your seed up in the way they should go. One of my concerns was in having a teenager at home (my daughter), who was in need of godly council and leadership at that time. I have seen many areas of my baby's life that would have crashed had I not been there to pray for her, to talk with her, and to help her understand her responsibilities at that time. I truly thank God for His love and kindness toward us, for teaching me that *His* ways are higher and far better than what I wish for at any time.

Remember: "Delay is not denial." Once again, this comes down to preparing ourselves, as mentioned earlier. God wants to make sure that we do not sink in any area of our lives. Yes, our children are a great responsibility but they should never be the excuse for why we stop trying.

If that were the case, I could have used all three of my children as an excuse —claiming 'They have their own destiny to fulfill'— and believe me all three were happy to move out! (*Lol*) There were rules they had to follow up in our camp and each one was for their own good. As with many children, they never liked it [strict discipline] then, but grew to appreciate it later.

Many single parents out there have achieved their highest goals, and many of them have more than three children, so I would not dare begin to complain. To be very honest, I was either too lazy to do something about it or did not have enough knowledge (neither was I searching) to pursue certain goals outside my comfort zone. My faith was so small, I was afraid to do anything —stuck and afraid equals a hot sticky mess! That day is long gone!

Again, as I shared before, I was looking for God to hand everything to me on that silver platter —after all, I was His daughter and any father wants his daughter to have the best. True as that is, most fathers know there are lessons that their children must learn in order to be productive in life. Until I started pursuing what HE put in my heart to do, nothing was happening. I changed my attitude: If it was to write a song, I wrote it. If it was to write another page of this book, I began doing so. I realized that each moment was ever so precious and important not only to me, but also to my Father, and to those that will catch this vision and run with it. God is making *Kingdom* connections; He is calling us to play our part.

Again, this goes back to the fact that someone is waiting on you —yes, you! — and you alone! You are the one sent to make your mark in their heart. Your responsibility is to seek God; ask the Father what is it He would have you to do, where He would have you to go, what He would have you to say. When He gives you the answer, let nothing get in your way; just do it! Start somewhere; God will take over and help you. I am a witness. Even now as I pen these words, I know it is His Spirit guiding me in putting them down for you.

I am encouraged to know that we have recovered it all. Everything taken from us —and I mean everything, including our joy, our peace, our happiness —all ours for the asking— restored! We shall not stop until God says it is over.

The Sound of Abundant Rain

You may have experienced the greatest loss in life,

Trouble surrounding, attacking your might;

The tunnel seems darkest, more than night itself,

Your throat aching from cries of desperate help.

Hope again, your cries have been heard,

Sing again, like the sound of the mocking bird!

Melodies reach the heavens and its pearly gates,

The rain has come; rejoice and celebrate!

An outpouring of blessings and healing to gain,

Listen! — There is the sound of abundant rain.

(Joel 2:23)

Testimony of Encouragement
(The Sound of Abundant Rain)

Has your life been on hold? Does the word "drought" sound like an understatement? Well, get ready, the rain is coming! I opened my Bible to I Kings 18:1 and was stuck on the words "I will send rain . . . ." From just that one phrase, I derived this poem —what do you say to that! The Lord must have heard my cry; for I have been crying out to God, so hard . . . neighborhood dogs howling at the train and fire trucks had nothing on me!

Know this: There will be times when our lives are at their best and times when we do not know where or how the next move will be. In those times, stay connected . . . allow God to continue to lead; you will be all right. Remember that it is all for your good: *"For I know the thoughts that I think toward you, says the LORD, thoughts of peace and not of evil, to give you a future and a hope"* (Jeremiah 29:11). Keep that Scripture handy; meditate on it.

I finished reading I Kings and then laughed so hard —because Elijah was no joke! He believed God and he had a true relationship with God. Elijah had faith and confidence in the wondrous working power of God. When the *true* prophet of God mocked those false prophets (idol worshipers) of Baal, I laughed until I cried —the Bible is so good! "What did I get out of reading those passages?" you ask. This: God was then and God is now still faithful to His Word and is definitely serious about seeing His will accomplished in the earth.

Pause a moment now to think of all of the patriarchs that have gone on before us. God did not fail them and He will never fail us. There is light at the end of what you may be facing today.

After defeating and killing the false prophets, Elijah told his servant to go and look at the sky, over and over again (seven times in all), until his servant came back reporting that he saw "a cloud as small as a man's hand." It may seem as if what you need may not be coming or may not be coming in the way that you thought it should. It may even look small right now, but wait! That rain started pouring down and — Oh my goodness! — so much, so powerful! That is just how God is going to rain down in your life.

My suggestion to you is that when the rain comes in your life let it pour down upon you. Then when you have received your blessed outpourings, make sure that you share with someone else. Amen.

Much too Good!

This morning God spoke about you,
Whispered your name and told me what to do.
You are so great and yet precious, too,
So much that He wants the best . . . .

He is calling you out of family traditions,
Speaking your name in heavenly positions,
Telling your heart to stand up and listen.
You cannot settle for what is less.

Calling you closer in relationships,
Making you wiser and more positive,
A prosperous life He wants you to live,
If only you make the decision.

How do you decide what is right?
Be the best husband— care for a wife?
How can I turn wrong into right?
Just look up and pay attention.

Open your eyes to what is spiritual,
Let go of affairs that steal your miracles.
Be blind to religious rituals . . .
Your season is at hand.

Be brave enough to take that step;
Even if you feel there is nothing left
It is better to have started than to regret.
You must believe that you can.

Remember not to move in haste —
You are much too good to go and waste
Your time
Your mind
Your life!

(Matthew 12:35 NKJV)

Testimony of Encouragement
(Much too Good!)

I wrote that poem for a particular colleague of mine; he is such a wonderful person, inside and out. 'Sisters' who are single, please hear me on this one: I wish to reach out to all of my brothers, whether black, white, yellow, brown, red, or green —you choose a color. 'Brother,' let me encourage you: I asked God to let me be a vessel that He could use and He has made me His instrument. Now is the time and the season and this is one of those moments I believe God will use me greatly. As I stand on my post, God has downloaded this word for you.

Please stop looking for solutions —you are the solution, my brother. "What do I mean?" Well, I am glad you asked. God created you so wonderfully 'great.' Yes, you, my friend, you with the beautiful eyes, you with the overalls, and you wearing that designer suit. God made you in His image (exactly how He sees you, not how you may view yourself).

What God wants is for you to look up and pay attention. Draw nigh unto Him and He will draw nigh to you; do not be afraid to come to God or, for some, to come *back* to Him. God is and has been patiently waiting for you to make that move. He absolutely loves you just as you are; where you are in life is no secret to our all-knowing Father. For you unforgiving brothers, please move on —stop crucifying yourselves and others!

A few 'brothers' spoke candidly with me recently about having a 'right relationship'. . . I suggested that they first start with themselves. "Are you really ready to handle that great woman God has for you?" I asked. "Don't walk into anyone's life or into any position knowing that you are not prepared. Hear me when I say this, it will be more work than what you are ready for."

My son always heard me say to him that before he walked into the life of some woman, to make sure he had himself together first. I know that we are not perfect but we can do our best. Hey, she *is* someone's daughter! — most likely reared to be treated like a precious jewel. Neither they nor I want him to walk into her life offering *nothing*. A great man I know said, when a man walks into your life, it is to enhance, not to take away from it . . . Amen to that! When you walk into your desires be sure you already have prepared well for what you would do when you receive them.

I am a mother of three and I, for one, want what is best for my daughters and my son, as well as for me. I have always encouraged them to be their best in everything they do and now I am seeing the fruit of our prayers, our faith and belief. So, my brother, here and now I ask, "Do you need to take a little time out to work on you?" Maybe you are ready . . . or just maybe you need to work on your approach with women (or anyone you encounter, for that matter). Maybe you are 'too picky' about the size of a woman? 'Honey,' let me tell you something about that: When you take that sweet queen on the inside and love her into what you want to see on the outside, your life will be so, so full! Hey —'he-sha-com-in-in-a-honda!' —don't make me shout up in here!

Men, do not let your eyeballs fool you. I understand that, in general, you are more visual beings than women . . . but you may be missing your gourmet meal by trying to step into the fast food lane. Just because she is 'Size 2' does not mean she is the right fit! Now I am not knocking at all what you may desire; I am just saying that, for some, what you may really desire *and* need is hiding behind 'Size 16.' Start walking with her if you want to see that 'Size 2.' (Check out the film "Why Did I Get Married?" for a marvelous affirmation of this.)

Follow me here: True love has no discrimination. Ask your 'Big Brother' Jesus about when the men were ready to stone Mary, the whoremonger: After her salvation at the hand of the Lord, she turned out to be one of Jesus' greatest followers. Do you see what I am talking about? With that great love in you, you can make anything happen — anything! First, you must be able to love. I do hope that you are at that point in your life.

For so long some of us have been paralyzed by generational teachings and suffered many insecurities. My hat goes off to those of you who are not so bound, those reared in a wonderful, more secure, Christ-filled home —more power to 'yah'! I am very excited about that.

For those who were not, who still are experiencing generational issues — harmful generational 'curses' causing separation, and anger barriers —you know what I mean —straight up bondage! Lay those to rest with the ancestors, okay! Lay aside every sin and weight that so easily besets you (that holds you back from doing what you know is right). Stop playing with past hurts! Please, do not misunderstand— some teachings received were the greatest, so do not go off on the deep end, okay! Hold on to those.

One of our brothers-in-Christ wrote a song called "I Need You Now," which is such a powerful worship song. I listen to it during my meditation time with God. In many of his lyrics, he utters a plea to God to come close or closer, and that he would stay close to God. You can hear in his singing that this is real, that if God left, he would leave, too.

Another psalmist's "Secret Place" is a song of compassion, drawing us nearer in worship before God. Songs such as these make you want to hurry up to heaven! (*Lol*) Here is my point: Sir, if you desire to live, Jesus is the way, the truth, and the life. There is no other true way to live your life in this earth. Being a better man, husband, leader, friend, guide, or provider is not it. It is not in your talents or in how cute you look; it is only in Jesus. It all starts (and ends) with God.

If you do not know Christ personally, let me encourage you to pray this prayer now:

> *Father, Thank You for being God and never leaving me nor forsaking me. I am a sinner and I need You now. Your Bible says*

> *in Romans 10:9-10 that if I confess with my mouth the Lord Jesus Christ and believe in my heart that You raised Him from the dead, I shall be saved. I confess that He is Lord and I believe in my heart. Now I thank You for saving me. Amen.*

My friend, if you just said that prayer for the first time in your life, you are now **saved** — Hallelujah! The angels are rejoicing over you! I encourage you to find a great Spirit-filled church that ministers to your soul and spirit, one that will help you to grow in the Word of God, more and more. You will need a Bible if you do not already have one, for along with prayer the Word is your key to success . . . together they are your *relationship doorway.*

With these tools, you will win the woman, the success, the healing and everything that you desire. If you have not been in worship and fellowship, it is not too late to start. Now that you have been 'grafted in,' it is important that you stay connected to the true vine, Jesus. God knows what is best for you (and He will cut away all that is not); after all, He created you, and you are created in His own image.

The most exciting thing to see is a man who loves God and his family, a man who knows what truth really is. That is a man that every woman wants and needs.

How Did I Get Here?

I started on this journey searching for real love,

Real truth, real everything

I really did not know how to get to the end.

Someone said I should start with me, so that is where this journey begins.

To start with me there is so much, you see

The hurt I let go of and let it all out

The pain and suffering I had to talk about . . .

The "Whys?" and "How comes?"— questions like that

Skeletons in my closet could knock you out flat!

Regrets — I had so many

Temptations and invitations I can count down to the penny

But wait! There was a RIGHT turn that I took on this road

It led me to salvation and lightened my load.

So much lighter my way — much brighter, my faith — much higher!

I began to see —Yes, I could see the deep inside of me

Oh, God, how I needed to be free! I will to be free. I am free!

No more spirit of confusion — messing up my mind with ungodly delusions!

Peace belongs to me, my joy belongs to me . . . Can you not see?

It is He — the WONDERFUL CHRIST — who made me free!

I am staying with Him right here in this place

No more fear, anxiety or disgrace

The question you ask, "How did I get here?"

I surrendered all.

(Romans 10:9, 10)

Testimony of Encouragement
(How Did I Get Here?)

Scrambling through the thoughts in my mind and trying to find the words to say to you, I will begin by saying, "Let Go!" Let go of all of the past; let go of all the anger, and let go of all that "stuff" that keeps you looking back! Let go of all you are trying to hold on to or that which is trying to hold on to you. Get it out of your system and move ahead.

The first thing I had to do to be free was to confess my faults to the Father (Heavenly Father). I cried it out and walked it out one-step-at-a time, day by day. The Bible says that, *"If [I] confess my sins, He is faithful and just to forgive [me] and save [me] from all of [my] sins"* (I John 1:9, insertions mine). One thing after another piled up on the inside; failed relationships and bad choices, drugs, sex, and whatever else one can imagine. God forgave me!

I remember many of nights cuddling up with a large bag of potato chips, trying to ease the loneliness or hurts from a man who said he would always love me, or from those so-called friendships that ended in betrayal. I not only had "little pity parties" but "big fat" ones —gaining weight out of control! I thought that I would not survive those wounds, but I did . . . I am still standing, and, guess what? —you will, too.

Now you must learn to forgive . . . forgive yourself first, and then others. "How?" you ask. Have faith in God to forgive (see Mark 11:22). God forgave me and I am living much better because of it —I know it, I see it, I feel it. I know you want to be free, also. Whatever your dilemma or stronghold, nothing is too hard for God! Confess the Lord Jesus, and you shall be saved.

"Saved from what?" you may be asking —from a life headed down the road to destruction and Hell if you do not change! Yes, I know what it is like to desire material things — money, cars, houses, clothes, and oh, please do not leave out the shoes! Hear me well: I was not born into money; we were welfare recipients, honey —and may I add, almost for forever! In fact, food stamps should have had our family's portrait on them!

I was under attack so much in my flesh, wanting and never achieving, always looking for external fulfillment. Guess what! I never found fulfillment in that lifestyle and neither will you. That is not why you and I were created (pleasures in and of this world), we were created for purpose and praise. Our Creator declares us "*fearfully* and *wonderfully* made" (see Psalm 139:14).

Not only had God made us in His image but He also purposed us into this earth to offer up ourselves as a living sacrifice to Him. One day you will look back on all that He has brought you through with a smile, a cry, or a laugh, forever remembering that He did it —God got you to that place of rest —and you and I both know that only God can!

Seek Ye First

Seeking ye first the Kingdom
Isn't something you're searching for;
It starts from within your heart
And continues to draw you more.

Hungry and thirsting for righteousness,
You're chasing after the One.
With each step you're drawing closer
Than when you first begun

A relational encounter that leaves you wordless
In a place where you're surrounded
By the beauty of His love;

So, if at all you are wondering . . .
The Kingdom, do you possess?
Looking into your mirror
Will put you to the test!

(Matthew 6:31-34)

Testimony of Encouragement
(Seek Ye First)

One of my favorite verses is Matthew 6:33: *"Seek ye first the kingdom of God, and his righteousness; and all these things shall be added unto you."*

For so long I have looked at this Scripture from a material viewpoint. I have embraced it, memorized and quoted it. I believed that by seeking God, all that I asked for was 'a given' —wrong heart!

After all, God did give us Jesus, did He not?

Well, I had to speak to 'Self' and 'Self' answered, "Yes, God does desire to give, and give, and give . . . but my perception of this Word was totally off base." I learned that seeking the Kingdom is more about God than you or me. God in return makes it about us. Let me explain.

As we begin to hunger and thirst after God, we become filled. We begin to pray more, to worship and devote our lives to Him. As we continue in obedience to God, He in return reveals Himself to us more, and more, causing us to begin seeing who we really are and why God created us in the earth. We then recognize that we are not persons just hiding behind money, houses, yachts, cars, or even the Bible. As God peels away our past, He develops courage within us, strengthens our will to rule with authority in the earth and shows us how to pursue peace. Although material things are a part of God's plan for us, the real Kingdom lies within, and nothing compares to the freedom that brings!

I want to have 'Kingdom living,' don't you? Well, now you know what to do —

Matthew 6:33.

What Are You Waiting For?

Do you understand how they had to fight?
Just for you and I to have the same rights

To lay down our heads and sleep good at night
To walk the same halls as the black and the white

Get yourself up get into the groove
Listen to me, I am talking to you

Acting the part just won't get you through . . .
It takes more than that. You know what to do

We are covered from his lies and treacherous schemes
He has no right to come in and still our dreams

Think back on the days when they marched it out
Shouted it loud, standing so strong . . .

Together and proud with so many in it to the end
Not just for them but for Judy and Kim

Even me too—
And especially you!

So where are you going Ray-Ray, Jaquan,
Lisa, Teresa, Katie, John?

You, too, Kyle and Dwayne
Life is still moving and people are proving again, and again

We can all do it
When we put our hearts to it

Will you be willing to change
When change comes to you?

Don't let your dreams just fade away; make them happen

Get up and get to it!
You know what to do—
Go on and just do it!

(II Timothy 1:6, 7)

Testimony of Encouragement
(*What Are You Waiting For?*)

I recently watched a documentary of a great man's life, and all I have to say is "Wow!" He fought a good fight, a courageous fight of faith, and so did those who marched with him. I often wonder if I could have endured all that they endured and still have integrity about it all. NO! I will not even begin to lie . . . the truth shall make me free. (*Lol*) God knew whom to use . . . and were they ever anointed to do what they did!

This goes back to my earlier statement about getting up and not letting anything stand in your way. I believe that when something comes back to you again there is in it a great message, which is this: Procrastination is hurting you! I decree right now, that you have deliverance from not paying bills on time, not returning phone calls, or not picking up the receiver when creditors call. You and I operate in excellence.

The truth, which I had to learn, is that creditors would not call if I paid on time. Remember to 'owe no man' anything . . . so answer that phone and talk . . . .

Get some kind of agreement started to clear that debt. (I am talking to myself while addressing this to you.) This is what I had to do. Today I am determined to be faithful over 'few things' because I truly want to be ruler over 'many'— don't you? Well, freedom starts one-step-at-a-time.

I wrote a letter to my creditors informing them of my financial situation and promising to send a small amount (a very small portion) toward my debt. I figured that they would appreciate me trying to do *something* rather than doing *nothing*. I want to be accountable for my actions. However, I believe many folks do not want to grow up; they are comfortable staying stuck in the same pattern of life year after year. Just look around. Is it getting better or worse? Too often you hear, "I'll just keep things the way they are." or "If it's not broke, don't fix it." Wrong! It is already 'broke' and God does not want us 'broken' or 'down and out' in life; so, let's get up and get to it!

One thing for sure, time is not waiting on anyone. Therefore, we must stop wasting it! Whatever it is that has distracted you from what God has put in your heart to do, be quick about it and get it accomplished; you are the one who will have to give account of what was done in your life, not what was standing in your way. You are the one who will have to sit and see others achieving their dreams while you sit on the sidelines. You are the one who will have to see generations live through choices made and the consequences when you refused to move with what God put inside of you.

GET IT or THEM OUT of YOUR WAY! What are you waiting for? We do not have time; it is passing by. Now with that said, remember that you can do all things through Christ who strengthens you (see Philippians 4:13); that you are more than a conqueror through Him who loves us (see Romans 8:37). There is so much to do . . . and generations are waiting . . . . Get up and get started now!

It is Your Season

It is your season, now seize this moment!
You have the reason, hurry up and get on it
Yesterday is gone. Don't waste another minute
So much to be done and it has your name in it

All that you need is set in its place
Waiting for you to come fill in that space
Dreams and desires that flow through your veins
Burning with fire, pouring out like the rain.

The promise is ready and given to you
Get up and get going . . . you know what to do
No longer just sit, nor listen to reason . . .
Your future is waiting
Now go! It is your season!

(Leviticus 26:3-13)

Testimony of Encouragement
(It Is Your Season)

Get up, and get your life back! In another one of my poems, I talked about not missing your moment; apparently, God really wants to get this message over to you. It may be that you do not know how to get started —just go ahead, dive in! Sometimes our nerves can get a grip on us; what you need to do is tell those nerves to sit down, take the back seat. Sometimes it may be our reasoning; do the same thing with reasoning, too. I do not care how old you say you are; that does not matter with the Lord. I encourage you not to let anything stand in the way of your future. Go back to the Bible and read about the men God used, especially brother Moses (see Exodus through Deuteronomy).

Remember, what God has for you is for you; but also know that if you choose not to obey the Lord will use another who is willing. He does choose to use you for what He has planned, but if you are not willing, our Father will not force you to do anything against your free will. Let me say here that I know the feeling of 'missing out' on what God wanted for me, and it was not a good feeling! It took years for what I missed to come around again. Thereafter, I made a promise to myself that I would never again be afraid to 'move on in life.'

I look at my children and think about my love for them, how much of an easier life I desire for them to live. It is never my desire to see them straining or stressing to pay anything. Although they have been okay in that area for the most part, I admit that they have had their moments.

Finally, I think about King David, that he followed his destiny, having both courage and faith. David the father produced greatness for his son Solomon, and King Solomon became one of the richest men of all time.

Go! Get your destiny!

Be Made Whole

I won't tolerate the lust of this flesh

Awaiting the very moment it would arrest me, caress me.

Why is it that when I want to do good, evil always is present with a force?

Coming at me, asking that I divorce

My first love — God the Father.

Why bother me evil?

Even I have been dedicated and consecrated

A long time have I waited.

I won't and can't fall for your compromises and devices

For you asking me to give up my prize of Eternal life—

I don't think so! God has made me whole.

I have confessed my freedom from the slavery of you

I walk with the Lord; that is what I do.

I see you and I am stronger, no longer tossed by mere deception

I will not give in to your trap and reap the repercussions

— It's all a lie!

Evil, you had a grip . . . And in my mind, I started to slip

Causing my flesh to trip — But God!

(Selah)

God, your hands there catching me before the fall, speaking to my very soul

Telling me not to let go but hold to the Solid Rock

That Rock who made me whole —

That Rock is JESUS!

(Romans 12:1)

Testimony of Encouragement
(Be Made Whole)

It is amazing how God loves us! Do you ever think about what we could have become if God had not stepped in to save us? 'OMG!' (My daughter always says that.) I do think about it a lot and right now I must rejoice —as a matter of fact, I put my praise right there! He is such a wonderful Friend, Father, Comforter and Savior. We could still be doing those same old things —over and over, and year after year —but God, in His amazing love through Christ, has given us a way of escape from all of that.

If you ***are*** still doing the same old things, over, and over, over, and over, over, and over, and —okay, I think you get my drift. That is exactly what it is like, so stop already! You are producing fruitless living and that is not the way to live. Do not delay your destiny any longer by continuing in this sinful way.

The word **insane** is described (my paraphrase) as "doing the same thing over and over and expecting different results." Are you insane? NO! Repeat after me: "I am not insane." There came a time when I had to ask myself this question. Looking in that mirror, I said, 'Terri, how long are you going to live like this? How long are you going to go around **this** mountain?' Like me, you, too, must **refuse** to live like that again. You also must tell yourself that you are much too valuable —that change has come, now!

Remember, change, times, and seasons will come whether you or I are ready for it or not. Do not miss it! (I almost did.) God desires to give us the desires He planned for our hearts; after all, He does know what is best. Meditate on Psalm 37:4: *"Delight yourself also in the LORD; and He shall give you the desires of your heart."*

It is true that many of us have received the desires of our hearts, yet we are not really living a life of completeness. What do I mean? Here is an example: For nine years, I worked a great job, one that I prayed to God for, for a long, long time. The best part of my job was the favor given me, and oh, I cannot leave out the pay, which exceeded my imagination and skills.

Each day I had the opportunity to meet and work with so many wonderful fellow believers from all over. I really enjoyed my position and even greater than that, I received a promotion to a new position, also undeserved! 'Lawd'!

Each night I went home to three loving children who made me laugh so hard I had stomach cramps. Yes, there is a "But" to this: Because I was not mature enough in the truth of God and His Word —let me say that again —the truth of God and His Word, I experienced several setbacks. It really does not matter your educational degree, your nice clothes, or your good smelling self; if you are not prepared, forget it! My ignorance and immaturity caused many challenges for my family and me, including the loss of our home.

Being made *whole* is more than getting the desires of your heart; that is not *wholeness*. Being made whole is an internal promise of the Father; the renewal of your spirit and enjoying a right relationship with God and His Son Jesus Christ. Secondly, it is our response in obedience to His Truth, and I am not talking about the repetition of prayer or the tradition of going to church week after week, or day after day; that is only a part, my friend. I am speaking of a righteous lifestyle. Where is our heart with God? We must have *that* relationship right first.

For my part, I was dream chasing and not being a God chaser. I was not hungry for *Him* —only for what I could get from Him. But now! God has allowed me to experience Him in such ways that I cannot even explain through words —I can only express it with love. Nothing gets in my way of worship now; no distraction of things or people can get in my way anymore. I will not let it! And you know something? —I am so much happier.

Are you?

I may not possess all of the material things I desire yet, but one thing I do know is that the peace of God rules my life, my decisions, and my heart. I have the key to wholeness and His name is JESUS.

Will you be made whole?

Will you allow God the chance to show you how great you are beyond your "nine-to-five" position or day-in, day-out routine?

He can do it . . . He promises in His Word: *"That if you confess with your mouth, "Jesus is Lord," and believe in your heart that God raised him from the dead, you will be saved. For it is with your heart that you believe and are justified, and it is with your mouth that you confess and are saved" (Romans 10:9-10 NIV).*

I wanted to be 'made whole' . . . and now I want to experience the greatest that God has for me. I am so thankful that God loves me enough to turn my messes into miracles.

BE MADE WHOLE!

Daddy

Talk to me . . . Walk with me. Don't you know I need you?
Laugh with me, cry with me; this is what you would do.
Chastise me. Surprise me. Can't you see I am waiting?
Where are you? I can't see you; your face is slowly fading.
I hear your voice and I smile, imagining you are here.

What's going on? — It has been a while . . . I miss you and I forgive
Memories take your place. Do I ever cross your mind?
So many times, I see your face and wonder, "Do you see mine?"
You are the one, the only one I want to hold my hand—
Catching me when I fall . . . helping me to stand.

To every father taking time to be there for your child:
May our God exalt your life and abundantly multiply!
Thank you, for your committed heart, fine examples you displayed.
Even if the times were hard and you wanted to walk away, but stayed!

And to the man who made the choice to leave your child alone:
God forgave you, and so did I.
So Daddy, come back home!

(Malachi 4:6)

Testimony of Encouragement
(Daddy)

I remember it as if it were yesterday: My youngest daughter Tierra and I were in church; she was sitting opposite me with her best friend Ishaiah (I-shay-yah). It was Father's Day and our pastor was at the end of his sermon, speaking about fathers. He passed out white roses to the children to give to their fathers seated in the congregation and asked that the children of those fathers come and stand beside them. When he finished speaking, my little Tierra (about 8 or 9 years old then) rushed into my arms and wept so hard that it hurt. Her very words were "Mommy, where is my daddy? I want him here!" I cried for her softly, not wanting to interrupt the pastor's benediction, and whispered in her ear how sorry I was for what she was feeling and going through at that moment, but 'Daddy' was not going to be there. Whew! I was so hurt. I wanted to break off into 'in-cre-da-woman' and find that 'brother'!

After service, I explained to our pastor what happened, so he talked with Tierra and loved on her a bit before we left. The ride home was a most tearful and difficult one because all three of my children were feeling the same way. My only thought was to show them the love that Christ had shown me through those moments when I grappled with thoughts of my own father. We are all still healing today from the wounds of not having our fathers in our lives; it takes a long time to let go. I never thought that I could heal, but I am . . . and my prayer is that my children will, too.

Can you see the cycle here? The enemy has worked so hard to destroy homes from the beginning of time, starting with Adam and Eve (see Genesis 3) —all the way down to our generations. Oh yes, but the greatest news is that there was a plan —JESUS!

Although their fathers have not been a physical presence in their lives since our relocation to Georgia, I have encouraged each of them to write to their children, to call, and to help whenever possible.

It is a blessing to have my daughters and my son. As a female, the hardest part of being a single parent to a young man is that you sometimes do not understand what he feels — times when you just have to allow him room to express himself. Hear me when I say this: It has been particularly hard to watch my son grow up without a good male example in his life. Yes, he and I would talk about life in general, and at times we talked about his growing up without his dad —he did not like it at all. I honor his openness and am glad he shares his heart with me, which has produced some very rewarding moments, as well as some very hard ones. I have seen my only son struggle in areas I knew only a man could teach . . . though the power of prayer has helped us through many such challenges.

Listen to me and believe me: The design of 'parenting' is that both parents be in the home. So to those of you trying to keep or hold your children from their fathers: Do not! —not unless you are certain they are being put in harm's way. You must not do so out of your own selfishness; it only causes greater harm. (Someone needed to hear that.)

As always, God has His "ram in the bush." Mine was a great man from my church here in Lithonia who helped to encourage my son on his journey through high school, and beyond. Isaiah is a better pianist because of this man (I will not reveal his name because he is a good man and I might come back and look for him myself. —*Lol*). Throughout high school, Isaiah struggled badly but the great part is that he made it! I am so proud of him —YOU GO BOY! I am most grateful to my 'church brother' for taking out time to spend with my son; for helping him shop for cologne, or nice clothes that made him look and feel distinguished —things that helped Isaiah's confidence and allowed him to see beyond where he was physically. Isaiah saw greater and better things and the two discovered a common bond —music. Although through the years, my son has made some choices that displeased me, God has been faithful to keep him through it all. Such things happen in life. Just have faith in God!

It has always been my desire to have a father for my children; and to avoid any misunderstanding, let me state that Isaiah's father was a part of his life as a young boy, but that was it. They have communicated from time to time, but nothing serious. I pray for their healing.

A word of wisdom: Please be careful about who you let in your life. I have had some characters in my lifetime! —have had to apologize to my children for my poor choices. I told them that the curse stops here: My seed will not endure the single-parent home syndrome or the teenage pregnancy "Who's the daddy?" drama, or the "Baby-Mama" drama. They are the "Chosen Generation," the "Royal Priesthood" (see 1 Peter 2:9). My offspring remain connected to the Vine. Never let it be said that our children are a lost cause because there is no father or, for some, no mother in the home. Always encourage your sons and daughters; show them and help them to know who and whose they are.

Fathers or mothers, if you have fallen away from your responsibility, get back up again and get in that race! My "spiritual father" told us to 'start from where we are'; let that now be your beginning. May God bless all fathers and mothers who are trying, but, for some unfortunate circumstances, are unable to reach out to or see their own children . . . my prayer is that our Lord will send you your miracle.

Isaiah 60:1 says, *"Arise, shine; For your light has come! And the glory of the LORD has risen upon you."* We proclaim Jesus as our Lord, and that with Him all things are possible. We have the victory!

Remember this White Boy

One morning I ran as I usually would do

Wanting to give up after that mile or two

My legs felt punished . . . my heart was through

But as I kept running, I heard God say

'Look in front of you; hold up your head.'

There was a white male walking just ahead.

God spoke to me, 'Tell him what I said.'

And as we passed meeting eye to eye

I spoke up to say, 'Young man, it's alright.'

And his reply took me to the moon

'You keep on running; it's alright for you too.'

And if ever a day you feel that you can't . . .

Remember, this White Boy said that you can.

(Hebrews 12:1, 2)

Testimony of Encouragement
(Remember This White Boy)

Wow! I am not kidding but his words blew me away that morning —or should I say that God did! The Bible says that God's ways are not our ways, nor are His thoughts ours; they are so much higher. It is up to us to obey what God is telling us to do. You might be the one who receives the blessing, just as I did.

So many times —I do mean *many* —I would start something and never finish; I would just quit in the middle of it. It was so frustrating! Help me, 'Lawd'! It always seemed that I would have to come back to that same place again. I must admit that I became afraid to get anything started because of my fear of failing or quitting. Has anyone ever been in that place before? Well, if you have, then you know the effect, how it paralyzes you. We must decide that we will get back up anyway until we succeed.

I took that step; now you take that step. I asked God to be with me, to help me succeed every step of the way; now you ask God to be with you, to guide your every step. Guess what! — He will. There will be challenging moments for sure, for if we live in this world there will be moments when you want to give up but you must keep on pushing. Let me add that whenever you make a decision to do what is right, evil will be present. Oh, you had better believe it! There is no way Satan is going to take your success lying down; he is going to give it his best shot to stop you, he wants you to throw in the towel. He wants you to murmur, complain and make excuses as to why it cannot be. Do not give him any excuse, okay!

Remember to ask God to help you to accomplish any and every task. All I had to do was make that first step, and God took over. There were for sure those times when I talked myself out of what I knew was right, and felt it later. Let none of us do that.

I have often had to reflect on what that young man said to me that early morning. Maybe someone has said something that sparked your interest or 'lit a fire under your feet.' If so, get up! — the rest is now up to you. That young man's response to what God spoke shocked me, because I thought I was the one who was supposed to be ministering, yet *he* turned around and gave *me* a word. Now, that is something! Isn't that just like God! (This is also the title of one of my favorite songs.) God will send you to people and places just to remind you that He heard your prayers, Hallelujah!

Think about this: Had I not taken the step to get up and try I would have missed it all. Do you understand? This is your time and it is your season; waste not another minute of regret, or another opportunity. Do not miss the blessing that God has for you. That young man's words continue to go the distance with me, for I continue to get up and get out. Isaiah 54:17 says, *"No weapon formed against you shall prosper . . .*" So, the truth is we have already won this battle! It is up to each of us to decide when we will take our place in the race. The decision is yours: You can lie there, never do a thing but accept whatever life brings, or you can decide to get up and go for it —make life happen for you and generations to come. By taking it one-step-at-a-time with God, we move closer to our glorious destiny.

Catching Up with Me

Lying here listening to 'Oldies' with my girls,
Talking with my girls; taking advantage of every minute.
Thanking God for allowing this opportunity. . .
For all that He has planned for me in it.

Many of days have passed me by,
Missing the main ingredients and not knowing why.
Slowing down just a little, I'm stepping back,
Breathing in and breathing out, laughing at that,
Smiling at this and catching blessings almost missed.

Instead of running and rushing, I stop for a time,
Taking back and recovering all that is mine.
Closing my eyes to unhealthy thoughts,
Shutting them down — whatever the costs!

Soaking my toes and massaging my feet,
Manipulating the minutes of this temporary retreat,
This is my day and this is my time;
I am catching up with me and taking back what is mine:

My time
My health
My finances
My family
My ministry
My LIFE—
I'm all caught up!

(Proverbs 14:1)

Testimony of Encouragement
(Catching Up with Me)

Get ready! Go on out and get those toes done; allow somebody to take off a corn or two. Oh, do not even pretend your feet do not need refreshing! (*Lol*) I am just reminding you of how important you are to the kingdom and how much God wants you to take good care of yourself. There must come a time when you have to say 'enough is enough' and then stop and see about you. Step back if you feel stressed; it's not God's plan for you.

I love jazz and find that it really relaxes my mind the most of any music. Jazz allows me that 'me time,' if you know what I mean. However, one of my all-time favorite musical groups is the R & B group, *The Temptations*. I have watched the movie covering the history of the group probably about 50 times already. Whenever I am in a particular grocery store and hear their songs, my head starts bobbing and my fingers start popping. Then watch out —it's on! There is nothing like those 'old oldies'! (Does that show my age?) I visit that store quite often because I so enjoy listening to the songs they play.

It is so important that you take time out for yourself, that you take good care of *you*.

If you do not, who will? Shopping to good music is my outlet. What is yours? — a spa treatment? Maybe a quiet day at home (love those moments, too)? I have made the decision to love me first and now I am noticing how everything else is coming along.

I do not want to feel old before my time, do you? Yes, that includes saying 'NO!' to some things and someone. Ooh . . . felt that hit somebody right there! Yes, I said it, because I have been down that emotional road of 'Yes' when I knew 'No' should have been my response.

Okay, this might hurt some a bit but, yes, you will need to separate from family, friends and associates. That can be tough, especially when you love family the way we do. Listen, no one will take care of you as well as you can. You have one life and if pulling away from time to time is what helps you to live life better and in greater peace, then take that opportunity!

Have you ever found that you have had better thinking capacity when you were in total silence? I have. Even if you are just soaking your feet, lying on the beach, resting in bed listening to music, or just watching the ceiling fan, make it your own moment. Here is the message: *You* must take out time for *you*. You must take advantage of every moment; you need it. Believe it, or not, those around you need you to rest, too. So remember to love *you* first, for when you do that love spills over and out onto others.

Girl, Don't You Know Your Worth?

You are beautiful in every way
Who said you could not shine
Ms. fearfully and wonderfully made

Forget about that negative; dwell on all that positive
Spread your wings, girl; go on and live
This is your season and, oh yes, you are the reason

Look at your beautiful hair—nappy, straight or wavy
No one else compares with the look you carry, Baby!
Single sassy and free or you possess that ring
Go ahead, look in that mirror: It's you, you're the main thing

Juicy girl or thin—it really doesn't matter whatever size you're in
It's you; you have that swagger
What you have is so unique. Who else in time can compete?

Stand in that mirror and flirt with yourself
Go on and take *you* off that shelf, 'Ms Proverbs 31 woman.'
Girl, you must know your worth!

(Proverbs 31)

Testimony of Encouragement
(*Girl, Don't You Know Your Worth?*)

Sixteen years old and out in the streets of LA! It was hard —hard and crazy! I did not always want to be out there . . . and to top it off, I knew absolutely no one to help me get back to being a young woman again. There was once a time of innocence in my life. Satan's traps were everywhere, and I do mean *everywhere*. Oh, believe me, there were plenty traps . . . and I fell into them. Guess what!—nothing has changed; he is still using the same traps, especially men, money and sex, but with different faces.

Please do not get me wrong when I talk about men; there are so many loving men in this world who love God and live great lives. I am letting you know that the side I came down was not so. . . .

I did not know my worth at all . . . I believed 'messing up' and 'messing around' was just a normal thing. I never considered consequences, such as the multiple times being beaten up and misused as out of the 'norm.' My desire was to wear nice things and have money in my purse at whatever the cost, but do you see that I was selling my soul!—can you see that? Unfortunately, that road I was traveling had a heavy toll to pay. The Bible calls those who take this road "whoremongers" (see Hebrews 13:4 or Revelation 21:8). Let us be real about this! Mother always said, "Call an ace an ace and a spade a spade."

I traveled that road for quite a while and then one day just sat back and looked at the way I was living and saw that it was not very pretty. I felt empty, so very empty. I was suicidal, depressed, hurt, broken, bitter and misused, filled with so much low self-esteem. But God! God came to my rescue: God told me that **He** loved me more than I could even think and that **He** would mend all of my broken pieces. The problem was I did not love myself, and God wanted to show me how to do that. Oh thank You, Jesus! Pause while I put my praise right here!

God showed me a glimpse of my future and I desired change right then. I am so glad that God does not leave us nor forsake us; I do not know where I would be right now had He done so. I am so glad to have Him in my life. It is a true saying that when you *think* about all that He has done for you, your soul cries out "Hallelujah!" Oh, I can feel His love all through me right now.

Now my plan is to keep what happened to me at that age from ever happening to my daughters, and my son, for that matter. A girl friend and I talked with our daughters one night . . . what we heard blew our minds! What we discovered about their thinking — how they felt, especially about themselves, it had us breathing deep.

Do not be afraid to hear what your children have to say, parents. If you do not pay attention . . . Satan will make sure that someone under his command will, because he is out to steal our seed. We must pray; we must keep them covered under Jesus' blood.

Of course, she and I prayed before beginning our session with them, otherwise, I do not think we could have made it out alive. Some of what the girls shared nearly threw us both into shock! I believe that because we were not looking through our eyes but through the eyes of Christ, we were better able to handle what they spoke.

Raising teenage girls in this world today is no joke; for that matter, raising sons is not either —I have one, too. Clearly, the things our youth deal with these days are far beyond what you or I faced in our time. As I said before, make sure you are fully prepared and armored to hear 'real truth.' If you want them to be free and experience what Proverbs 31 talks about, you must be open. My friend and I want that for our girls, and I am glad she was there with me . . . also thankful our daughters had such a good connection to be open to share in front of each other. They shared their fears, challenges, and experiences, how they overcame and are still overcoming temptations. Someone, grab on to these nuggets!

Where do you stand with your children? Make it a point to spark a conversation; let them know that you are interested in their lives —that is what love is; and if you have made wrong decisions that have severed your relationship, get back up and in there! We are all growing in HIM and we all have 'short comings'; it is up to us not to give up. Our goal is to be the very best woman or man God has designed us to be, especially for the children He has given us.

We were able to sit down with our daughters and show respect for who they were as women, and vice versa. After that, we saw a greater confidence in them that was not there before, and today we have a freedom to trust them more because of that night.

God gave us that wonderful opportunity to talk openly about everything, and I do mean *everything*! I know it must have been stressful for them to hold all that in.

Our daughters are now college students and they will definitely encounter many different experiences along the way. We learned the only way to help them better understand their walk with Christ is to open up to them our own lives, how we made it through; therefore we talked for hours and *listened* to each other. It was amazing how free we all felt leaving that room!

Hear me: Our loving Father wants us to prosper in every way. Our children want to be something more than just regular, and that they are [more than "regular"] . . . they are spectacular at everything they do! We just have to continue to pray and profess the truth over them, for that which God has planned. It is up to us, parents, to lead them down that right path. God has given you and me the opportunity to lovingly minister to our 'Proverbs 31 women' and to our 'Proverbs 31 sons.' Are you delaying? Please do not!

Our children are crying out today for our help in so many ways and we have the answers. Yes, you and I have the answers, which is why God entrusted us as their parents. I assured my children that I am going to be all "up in their 'Kool-Aid'" until they are married, and even then I will check in from time to time. Like me, I know that you want the best for him or her. The question is what do they see in you that will make them want to be the best?

I pray that you will have the courage to sit down and speak wisdom to your child or children, and if you cannot do it alone, do as I did —make it a round-table discussion. Just make sure that God is at the head! I promise that it will be a breaking point in your lives. The end of this story is that we have wonderful 'Proverbs 31 women' (and men) who are going to make a godly impact in this world. No matter what we see, we continue to profess the best in their lives.

My Body Belongs to God

I use to think my body was mine,
Taking it wherever my mind would explore,
Running through people, places and time,
Abusing and using it more and more.

But I heard a message that captured my heart,
Causing my body to stand still:
It said *I AM* the temple of the living God,
My body to be used for His will.

Freedom from poor mentality,
From lack of knowledge, lack of wisdom;
Freedom from every binding curse and chain— every religious prison;
Freedom from drug and mental abuse, that ugly low self-esteem;
Freedom from the old that has passed away — Birth to a better me!
We only have one body— do not misuse it, abuse it or waist it;
Our body belongs to God.

(I Thessalonians 4:3-5)

Testimony of Encouragement
(My Body Belongs to God)

I know someone is out there that can identify with me: You, too, thought that you created yourself and did not have to answer to anyone. Well, allow me to 'burst your bubble' — you do!

Know that we are accountable for what we do to and with our bodies, what we put in them. That is why right is always right, because doing what is wrong to your body causes major problems —physically, emotionally, mentally, and especially spiritually. Our bodies are to be used and kept for God's purpose; that is what they were created for. Because of the indefinite number of distractions and momentary pleasures, many neglect their first responsibility, to stay spiritually healthy. A healthy state comes by feeding the mind, body, and spirit with the Word of God. I cannot tell you the number of times I neglected to do so . . . weeks on end . . . arising with no prayer, and no Word, missing the mark! So all of my old mess started surfacing, trying to creep back in to the opening I had created.

In Luke 11:23-24 Jesus talked about those who are *with* Him and those who are not. Demons possessed a man who was cleaned up and set free; however, because he did not seek a relationship in the Word (but only a 'temporary fix-up'), those demons returned, bringing even more demons with them to fill that empty space in the man's soul. Not only did he have to deal with the mess he had just gotten out of, he now had much more of it to fight off again. Can you see how Satan wants to keep you down, to wear you out? How can we keep serving something that does not mean us good?

Ladies, you may have left him once . . . because you had no relationship with the *real* Man, Jesus, you went right back . . . and this time all hell came against you, making it even harder for you to walk out again. I have been there, done that, won that trophy! Yes, I am speaking from experience; this book is definitely for me, too.

It is so important to involve God in every decision-making, especially when 'dating' (for those who so engage), because so many relationships have become hurtful, or even fatal, with the wrong approach or improper courtship. Know this: God is the 'Greatest Date' one could ever have! Intimate time spent with the Lord is matchless; there is nothing in this world like it. Don't you think that God would know who and what is best for you and when the time is right for you? Our challenge is that we feel or believe that our "biological clock" will run out before God fulfills His Word —NOT true! That is a trick from the pit of hell — do not believe it! God is Keeper (to those who want to be kept), and I am a living witness to this truth. How about you?

If you are still debating leaving a place of abuse, allow me to encourage you a little more: GET OUT NOW! LEAVE IT ALONE —RIGHT NOW! You are the 'chosen people,' 'a royal priesthood,' 'a holy nation.' Yes, you are a 'peculiar' person, one set apart for God (see 1 Peter 2:9).

Stop allowing, yes, I said 'STOP ALLOWING' it! Make the decision not to tolerate it anymore; that includes smooth talkers trying to get you to do things that you know you should not be doing. Look at you! You are created for greatness — fearfully and wonderfully made! You are not the problem; the problem is that others do not know their own worth in this life and therefore want you down on their level. Do not dare go there; it is time to stand up for who you are and whose you are.

I would not have known that I could be *anything* had I never taken that first step to try. Why not do that now? You take that step. I have been at the point where you may be in life and I fell . . . but repented . . . got back up, determined not to go there again! My 'wanting' to make it turned into 'I think I can make it' and then to 'I know I can make it.' Truly, it is a process; it will not always happen overnight. Babies crawl before they walk and are given milk before given meat — right? Well, it is the same way with us, and our heavenly Father, Who must first see that we can handle where we are going, that it will not hurt us. God is a loving Father, One who wants to make sure that along the way, never are we damaged or abused.

Sometimes, someone gives us something beautiful in life, but because we are not prepared to receive it, we misuse or handle it improperly. Yet there is hope in that God is merciful and forgiving, for He gives us another chance, another opportunity for us to be faithful with the little . . . then He sees that we can be trusted over much. Listen, we only have one body, so do not waste it. For those of you who do not yet know who you are, I ask that you repeat this prayer of repentance with me:

> *Father, thank You for life . . . Thank you for Jesus, Your Son, who came to die for me, who was buried for me and arose for me so that I could live. I accept Jesus into my heart, right now! Thank You, Father, that I am made in your image, that I am created for YOUR pleasure. Lord, help me to know this more and more each day. Right now, I dedicate my life to You, to love You, and to serve You. Thank You, Lord. Amen.*

Praise the Lord for your life! The angels are rejoicing!

Spirit of Gluttony

I am in this race and crowned undefeated

Spirit of gluttony, you are not wanted nor needed

I have my plan and I have won

My body is a vessel of God's Kingdom

Once you had me captured inside my mind

I'm free from your spell and I draw the line

Greater is He that is living in me, so

I speak to you now: Be gone! — I am free.

Goodbye!

(Proverbs 23:1, 2, 6-8)

Testimony of Encouragement
(Spirit of Gluttony)

Is there anybody out there 'feeling me' on this one? — overeating! 'Lady T' was not for exercising and that was the problem: I have weighed up to 227 pounds, while making every excuse as to why I could not and would not lose weight. I could not because I did not want to be *committed* to what it takes to be healthy. It was hard to climb stairs without breaking into a sweat, panting heavily, okay, let alone trying to get into those cute jeans still hanging in my closet! Oh, and this is a good one: holding my hands in front of my gut line when a fine brother approached or walked my way, as if he hadn't already seen me before that moment.

As of today, I am working on improving my health first. Along with regular exercising, I have changed my diet. Exercise has been the big challenge, and although I get out and run a few days a week, it is my goal to do even more. Hey, if we do not love what we see, how can we expect someone else to love it? I have turned from the late night ice cream and cookies; they must no longer be a part of my plan because sugars cause me to blow up like a balloon in the gut area. How bitter sweet! Yes, 'bitter sweet.' It is time you, too, got up and joined a fitness center or made a plan to exercise daily. I am not saying that we all should look like supermodels. If you are a healthy 'Size 16' and loving it, keep on moving, honey! However, if you know that you are not (healthy, that is), then STOP! — Stop making it worse . . . get your hind parts up and do something about it!

My goal is to feel attractive and confident about my entire look; that is what I want for myself and that is what I am working toward. With that said, we must put forth the effort of making that happen. Instead of cereals with lots of sugar, I now intentionally look for something better. Be encouraged; there are so many different types of programs available; so make sure you find one that will work for you. Keep trying until you find what fits best. I am . . . . I am willing to try what is necessary and safe, not only to get the immediate results I want but also to live a long, full life. It is time to live and to live well!

What about you?

Many of you may be on medications that may cause bloating or you face other health concerns, so please seek your physician for advice. I am not a doctor. I *am* simply led to tell my story, so my goal here is to stop making excuses and to help you stop doing the same, year after year. It is time to make that change. You know that God has been speaking to you . . . (He ministers to me, too.) So get up and get going! We can do it. I am doing it. I look forward to seeing the new you.

I Forgot About Sorrow

I forgot about sorrow when you entered in.
I saw my tomorrow shining on your skin.
My troubles far behind me then;
A new horizon — I can see the end.

I forgot about sorrow being here with you.
Your presence transformed my grey skies to blue.
This is true love so exciting and new;
I forgot about sorrow the day I met you.

I forgot about sorrow and you calling me friend.
It's alright now to smile and live again.
I see my tomorrow I forgot about then.
I forgot about sorrow when you entered in.

(Proverbs 18:24)

Testimony of Encouragement
(I Forgot About Sorrow)

When I began writing this poem, two women came to mind. Although Jesus is always the inspiration for all of my writings, I want to share testimonies surrounding those close to me. One of those women is a girl friend in Jacksonville, Florida, the other in Oceanside, California. There is always something so sweet about their approach to encouraging me; God always uses their tongue as a writer's pen to say just the right words for every situation.

Isn't it amazing how sometimes we can connect with a complete stranger in the spirit? They can walk up to us, speak words of life to us, and we think to ourselves, "I know we must have met somewhere before." But really, we haven't. I often wonder how so many people could be so much alike and have such similar experiences, yet not know each other at all.

Well, one thing is for sure: I know and love these women. Without a shadow of doubt, I know that they care a lot about me, that they love me. There is such a peace and presence of God when I am with them. I am sure you also can think of someone (or two) who has your back, just as these 'sisters' have mine. If not, then we have to get you someone!

Let me tell you about my friend in Oceanside, who is such a prophetic woman. It is so remarkable! One minute we are talking on the phone and the next she has gone over in the deep on me . . . her husband will do it, too. Do you have someone like that in your life? Someone who will tell you what God says, whether you like it or not? That is who she and he are, and the wonderful thing about it is that they speak it with such grace.

I am amazed so at how God has fitly joined us together not only with Himself, but also with one another. We have so much in common that it is almost frightening; even our sons are like 'twins' in many ways: they look alike, act alike, and exhibit certain other similarities. Her two younger men are the absolute sweetest! Those handsome fellows make me feel like a celebrity every time I arrive. There is so much to say about her husband, whom I shall call "brother-in-law." (I need another book to share that story.) Although she and I are first cousins, we never had the chance to grow up together . . . still we act like sisters. The first time we met, we stayed up all night sharing our life stories, and I do mean 'all night.' We had to make the decision to go to bed —our bodies wanted to, we did not.

I realized that I had found my other 'me' and she said she found her other 'her'; almost as if we were birthed by the same mother (always knew I had a twin in the spirit somewhere). I love her so! We shared so much that night and discovered we had so much in common that it just blew us away!—especially our conversation on "the 3M's"— men, money and mind.

We shared so many deep things and precious moments and we cried and laughed together. What a healing for us both! My mom and her mom (biological sisters) declare that we are "two peas in a pod." I believe they are right. From that moment on it has been hard to separate us. It was hard to leave her that weekend and even harder now that we live thousands of miles apart. We have found ways to see each other, but I believe that when you find someone that you can relate to, long distance separation is always difficult. However, the greatest part is knowing that God loves us so much that He made someone for us to love, and someone to love us back . . . for me that 'someone' is 'Shell' and her family.

Have you found a friend yet?

Now for my friend in Jacksonville, Florida: You go, girl! I have known her about twenty-five years; we were roommates in Long Beach, California. We always talk and laugh about where God has brought us from . . . we know that we will never go back to that routine of living ever again. We have laughed and reflected on all that we did, concluding that we could have been dead. We did a lot of sinning, for which I repent. Oh, God forbid I should ever go back! Where would we be without God's grace and mercy? What would we do? Remember, God is not mocked, whatever we sow, we shall also reap! We pronounced crop failure on all that was back there and prayed with thanksgiving for God's merciful kindness.

What seeds are you sowing? What are you putting out there? Will you reap a good harvest?

My 'Ms. Florida' has a wonderful family. Her husband of eleven years is one of the greatest producers who is now in heaven; he just will not admit it yet. My friend encourages me continuously, cracks jokes with me, and expresses her love for me. We both are committed to moving forward in spite of what things may look, feel, or seem like. That should also be your stance. Remember to keep on pressing through the toughest moments even though they may seem to have no end. Sometimes the pain can be so tough that we lose focus, but know that the end really is near. Stay on the path and do not look back!

A great friend with the same positive mind in your life will help you make it to the moon if that is where you want to be. 'Ms Florida' does that for me, and I respond in the same way with her, which is how true friendship works. We love Jesus and enjoy sharing His love not only with each other, but also with others.

One day another friend of hers came by and we all sat down to breakfast. After eating, each of us left the table filled and encouraged in Jesus' joy; so much so that I received an unexpected blessing for speaking into her friend's life. God's power is amazing! One moment you can just be eating and the next, God drops a blessing on you. Oh, how I needed that blessing! "What?" you ask. While my Jacksonville friend was taking me to the airport for my return to Atlanta, she diverted and drove to her bank where she poured out another blessing on me. I never mentioned and did not have to say anything at all about my financial situation during that visit. God already knew . . . God spoke to her heart. She was excited about blessing my life, and I was excited to receive the blessing, thank YOU! What a friend! —has always been and I am sure always will be.

Let me repeat this: One thing about a real friend is that they tell you what you do not want to hear at times; therefore, the question becomes 'Can you or I handle it?' Know, for certain that if you give out love, love will be given back to you. I love *being* loved!

You never want someone around that is always going to agree with you. In spite of what you might think of them afterwards, you want —and need —someone who will agree with Christ and speak truth. As I mentioned before, it is *the way* my true friends ministered to me that made and still makes the difference. Please be careful how you bring God's Word across to people, so that you do not chase them away or drag them down, but draw them nearer.

Let the Truth Be Told

I've had rebellious days
Weaknesses in so many ways
Fallen down like never before
I've gotten up many times more
It was flesh that was speaking louder
Temptations of life had the higher power
The pleasures of sin stole my life away
Sinking in deep day after day
It wasn't until when I confessed
That it was me who created this mess
And no longer will I go on like this
From that day on, I decided to live
With the help of the one who most certainly saves
Who freed me from sin and my ugly ways
Now moment by moment I am gaining strength
I have overcome by that power within
If confession is truly good for the soul
Then obedience is better, if the truth be told.

(James 5:16)

Testimony of Encouragement
(Let the Truth Be Told)

I remember sitting on the edge of my bed, debating whether to go to church or stay at home because there was not enough gas to make it around the corner, and I had to take my sister back to the airport. We both were 'financially challenged' then. Well, the truth be told, I did not attend church that Sunday. My heart hurt so because I knew I needed to be there, yet I did not have the faith to go! I knew someone would have helped me get back home but that was the challenge, an on-going one most of the time —one that I was sick and tired of . . . I needed a change! I wanted a change! In spite of how disappointed I was in myself, I still sat down to write.

The job I worked only allowed me three days a week, at six hours per day, which added up to a mere 18 hours per week. Oh! Do not miss a day —being that there were four mouths to feed in my household! The hardest part was not being able to offer more than that to my children; lack was definitely our great challenge. What was I going to do? Panic sat in at first, but then I remembered to whom I belong. Is it not amazing that when Satan has any little way to invade your mind, he takes full advantage of that opening! Having repented, I began confessing that I was indeed a praying woman, a believing woman, a strong woman, and a professing-the-Word woman; so what in the world was going on? "Manifestation, come on in!" I said. Manifestation was there; it just took a little time for me actually to see it.

Sometimes we look at our situation in the wrong way, meaning that I had to stop and realize that I lived in a big beautiful home, paying 'less than nothing' a month, eating pretty well each day, with central air and heat running up and down the hallways, and free membership to a workout center on my job! Dressed to impress every time I step out the door, children in designer wear (whenever they wished to get dressed), and privileged to fly across this globe, even 'free' if I want! So why in the world was I complaining?

I am free and highly favored, with a boss who encourages me every chance he gets and children who are alive and well-productive citizens. Yes, it is a wonderful life. What then in the world do I have to complain about?

I believe this may be the answer: Sometimes we can get so distracted and overwhelmed with what we see, that we really do not *see* . . . . The psalmist David reminds and charges us: *"Why are you downcast, oh my soul?"* . . . . *"Lift up your head, o ye gates!* . . . . " (see Psalms 42:5a; 24:7a, 9a). The prophet Isaiah commands us: *"Arise, shine; for your light has come! And God's glory has risen upon you"* (Isaiah 60:1). Even in writing this book, I am receiving revelation of something God has just put in my spirit. Okay, you get my point!

It is all right to admit the truth about what is going on in your life; however, you must not allow the physical things of life to replace the spiritual, causing you to start condemning yourself. That in itself is another distraction to keep you from moving ahead. Thank God for forgiveness, and for the days made available to us. I am so thankful! I am getting the rest I need and the time now to put this book into action. I am accomplishing what I really want to be doing. Is that the case with you? What are you doing with the time given to you? Do take time out for yourself; we all need it.

The truth of the matter is that we will all face trials; how we handle them is what will make the difference. First Thessalonians 5:16-18 shows us how: *"Be joyful always; pray continually; give thanks in all circumstances, for this is God's will for you in Christ Jesus"* (NIV). That is not saying to be 'fake' . . . just saying that in *everything* (no matter how it looks or feels) give thanks, for this is the will of God in Christ concerning us. Make a choice to have joy —come what may!

Trials come to bring out the best and the worst. What do I mean? The worst is when you see all the fears, anxieties, and weaknesses, everything that had you bound. The best when you encounter great trials and find that you are still standing. You see how far you have come . . . strengths you have gained . . . more importantly, how much you have allowed God to take over. Now rejoice!

A cleansing of our past has to come so that our future will be *sweat-less*. Remember, at every new place there is new territory to gain. I want to grow up and expand my territory! Don't you? This means having to endure hard things as a good soldier and having to make new decisions that will not cause a repetition of old stuff. It also means these temporary moments in time are not to become lifetime hindrances, which they can if we allow it. Do not allow it; do not be stuck in the old way. Keep moving forward!

I have gained more, learned more, and become closer to *Abba, Father* in my journey. God knows exactly where we are in life and God knows exactly what we are up against before we get there. So let us allow God to do what He knows how to do best —fix our broken lives. Keep on moving through every trial, through every disappointment, and beyond even every victory. Yes, please do not stop there! Beware of self-deception; sometimes we can accomplish something good and think that it is so because we have a little money or status, believing that we 'have arrived.' No, we have not arrived! It is not about us in any way, form or fashion; it is about God, about His Son Jesus the Christ.

"Not Going Around this Mountain" is the title of a song I penned; it talks about not repeating the same things over, and over again. You, too, must find that place in life when you say 'enough is enough' and move on from there, never to look back!

Do not waste time! Time is precious or costly; it is something we will never get back so spend it wisely, as good stewards —the way God intended. Amen.

So Traditional

Be quiet! Hold up! Stop! Let us start over;
Don't take for granted this wonderful moment.
We have this day before our King;
Stay a while and slow down for a minute;
Let's reason together to see what is to be done.
Don't make this a pit stop or a fast food break;
Let us sup together, get to know one another.
You share and I will listen.
Your praise and exaltation will bring us closer together —
Closer in relation,
So take off your hat and scarf,
It's time for meditation.
I am always here,
I am willing to wait.
Because you're so exceptional,
Let's not make this so traditional.

(Romans 2:28, 29)

Testimony of Encouragement
(So Traditional)

Today was one of the most glorious days of my life! I had the honor of ministering in song at our church and we worshipped God as if we had lost our minds—it was awesome!

The message was entitled along the lines of "Knowing Christ, So He Will Be Known to Others." One of the most humble elders in our church ministry delivered the Word, and the most surprising thing happened: As she spoke, she began to cry. So moved was I by her freedom in the Lord that I wept, too.

I had never seen her break a tear before and many others will tell you the same. She is joyful and extremely funny, one of those who keeps up the excitement about living for Christ; there is always something funny coming out of her. One thing for sure, she loves God and I mean truly *loves* Him! Her passion to love on God is remarkable; everything she planned for that morning went right out the window as God rested on us there.

Such freedom is the kind that God desires all the time for us; He wants to take us to higher heights and new places in Him. We were all in and out of singing and praising; worshipping God so much that time no longer mattered! That only comes when we are spending quality time with our Father, and she was able to lead us into an extreme worship with God because she was already there in her spirit. It was a memorable moment, one that none of us has forgotten.

When you decide to make time for God, that same old routine goes right out the door. God is not looking for you to punch in and punch out; He desires *relationship*. He desires *truth*. Scripture declares it: "... *they that worship him must worship in spirit and in truth*" (see John 4:24). Thank you Elder, for keeping it real!

The Struggle that Has Been

Father, I asked "Why me? Why me?"

Why not you?" was the reply.

Because it seems every day has become a load to bear;

Those who surround me don't seem to go anywhere.

Ten years have gone by and it's the same ole, same ole.

Ten years down the line and I'm struggling a little more.

Where am I going? What is it to do?

This struggle is so long and I paid all of my dues.

I've tracked my money and counted the cost:

Peanut butter and honey— so much that was lost!

Living this way has challenged my mind

And losing my job came at the worst time!

Slow down; slow down, My child,

Take time out to think:

Did I bring you this far to let you fall or sink?

How strong would you be if you never had to try?

How could you relate if you never had to cry?

What testimony to give if struggle was not there;

Could you even comprehend? Or would you really care?

So why do you ask, 'Lord, why me?'

It is because you were chosen to give My name glory!

Embrace where you are . . . Give life your best!

It won't be ten years but eternity blessed.

(Isaiah 54:4)

Testimony of Encouragement
(The Struggle that Has Been)

If you are like me, waiting to see things 'come to pass,' don't fret! —you will. Just continue to trust Him! I use to say "Why me, Lord?" until I was almost blue in the face. Then my "Why me?" became "Please, not me yet, Lord!" I saw so many broken pieces to my life that I needed a miracle to mend every one.

It is amazing how desperation can cause you to question God or even lash out at Him. Oh yes, I have done that . . . and immediately, I had to turn around and R E P E N T. I know that God knows what is best for me.

In my past, I did not manage money well and had the nerve to pray to God to give me that big break making all this money . . . and for what purpose? —my own selfish gain? Then I would have been angry with God for losing it all. Now please, do not let me talk about praying for a husband, with all that excess baggage and bad credit trying to walk into his life —I don't think so! Although there are some who do . . . never realizing that without allowing God to work it out for our good, it will end in disaster. Help us, Jesus!

God is not going to send His best only to have it taken advantage of, especially when we show we have no idea how to be good stewards over what He has already placed before us. Please, be faithful over that "few" first, and the rule over "much" will come. I do not want just anyone, either; I want God's best! I definitely do not want my daughters, or my son, to stray back into the world when they have received the right to all heavenly blessings. We want to be able to keep our prizes, not throw them away. We must allow God to get rid of all the mess and to clean us up; that we will feel and look better. Believe me, if you take one step, God will do the rest!

Isaiah 40:31 declares, *"But they that wait upon the LORD shall renew their strength; they shall mount up with wings as eagles; they shall run, and not be weary; and they shall walk, and not faint."* God promised that we shall make it — and be revived in the process. Do you believe?

He also promised in John 15:7: *"If you abide in Me, and My words abide in you, you will ask what you desire, and it shall be done for you."*

Yes, I know about struggle . . . know there were many challenges but so were there plenty of joys, too. The Lord provided and we learned to appreciate where we were for that time in our life; we learned to lean not to our own understanding, but to trust Him to help us make it through every season.

Do you trust God?

Remember that your life is not just about you; God wants to take what you have and show others that with Him all things are possible. Your reading this book —birthed through my life struggle —is in itself a testimony.

Now there are two choices: (1) We can complain and stay where we are, or (2) We can choose to rejoice and make a conscious decision to be thankful in whatever comes our way. First Thessalonians 5:18 says, *"In everything give thanks: for this is the will of God in Christ Jesus concerning you."* If you have been making dumb choices and later having to deal with the consequences, STOP IT!

Listen to me: Be of good courage, for God is never surprised . . . He gives you victory even through all that . . . . Learn from those poor choices, and get back up! Your struggle is over!

Two 'Sistas' and a French Fry

Am I my Sista's keeper?
I most definitely am
We fit together like two frying pans
Through the laughter and through the pain
Through the sun shine and the pouring rain.

You make me laugh; I make you cry
We 'patty cake,' yell, and sigh
You make me cry and I make you laugh
My eternal friend forever — at last

We pray together and stay together
Always believing the best
You are the one who makes it better
But you feel I make it best.

I honor you most my 'sweet apple pie'
As we stand at our post —
Two Sistas
and a French Fry!

(Proverbs 18:24)

Testimony of Encouragement
(Two 'Sistas' and a French Fry)

This shall be the title of my next book, or movie, or play, or something — "Two 'Sistas' and a French Fry." Do you like that? Its basis is a true event that happened with a good friend and I. In my re-telling the story, you will see how God uses our trials to minister to the lives of others.

Have you ever had a friend or friends that made you feel like you were on top of the world, even though you knew that you were not? I have a few in my life I can think of and I will write about them a little later. One in particular is Angie . . . I am laughing right now just mentioning her name!

When Angie and I get on the phone together, it is a mess because we can laugh at so many crazy things. We both worked at a company located far north of where we lived.

I remember when we first met in her office that I was there testifying of God being my 'Keeper' . . . . (Angie admits today that she did not want to hear then what I had to say about God.) Then in one day, while at work, we both were suddenly without transportation because our cars were re-possessed!

I can laugh now because back then, just to think of it happening was so intense . . . but praise be to God! My car was the first to go . . . and at that time, Angie told *me* to 'keep the faith,' then we both went back to work. A few hours later, Angie's car was 'trucked' off the lot! What we encountered that day was a hot sticky, smoking mess! We both looked at each other and knew we had to do something quick —since earlier she had become my only ride home. I eventually reached a friend of mine, an Elder from my church, who picked us up, prayed for us and blessed us. And guess what? We made it to work for quite a while afterwards until Angie got another car. I did not get another ride right away (another story that I shall write about later).

I noticed that Angie would watch me a lot. She shared with me that she was not a faithful, church-going woman at that time, that she had her doubts. I believe that I was there to be that light to shine on Angie's path, to get her to turn fully toward Christ.

Who has God put in your path to minister to? What are you showing them about Christ?

I was (and am) so thankful God taught me how to trust Him. Angie and I had a few close encounters with struggle at that time but we still kept pressing forward in spite of it all. She was my blessing as well in so many ways; only God knew how much more confident I had become with someone like Angie walking with me through all of that . . . . Ecclesiastes 4:9, in essence, says that 'two heads are better than one.' How true!

If you are thinking about divorce, please take time to carefully consider what you are about to do. I am not saying to stay in a place where you may be harmed, but rather reach out to your pastor or brothers and sisters of the church if abuse is indeed going on.

What I am saying is that two walking together with Christ is so much easier than doing it alone. Believe me!

Now back to my story about Angie and my funniest, most memorable moment — our 'French fry' episode. This is a powerful testimony to us even unto this day; I call it "Two 'Sistas' and a French Fry."

Our tummies were growling so loud we could hear them over the radio. We were as hungry as all outdoors and, between us, we could only come up with about $1.50 to purchase a large box of fries. I was so hungry that Angie even looked like a big, juicy cheeseburger to me. I have no idea what I looked like to her —maybe a double-cheese! (We both could get down with some eating.) Well, what we decided was that since we only had about 30 minutes left on our break, we would sit in the parking lot, pull out the Bible, read Scripture, pray, and divide the fries between ourselves —one for me, and one for you. My friends, we really did this! Would you believe that by the time we finished eating, we were full! (Does *Jesus feeding the five thousand* sound familiar?) I kid you not; I know it may seem small to some but to us that was the greatest blessing this side of Heaven. God continued to show us how much He loved us and wanted to take care of us. Oh Lord, how we needed that reassurance!

These moments helped our faith grow and today we share that testimony with so many who may have grown weary, or even fainted in well doing. We have encountered many hard things after that moment. Did you hear me? I said 'moment.' I know it may look a little grim for you but when you allow God to come into it, that situation becomes a testimony to help someone else, and even for you a miracle.

Today, Angie and I pick up the phone and laugh at that moment; it brings us great joy along with a bunch of stomach cramps (from laughing). I am glad that God allowed us to be there together when we encountered those hard moments. I do not say that I am *glad* about that moment —be it ever so funny —because it was definitely challenging. Just know that God always has that 'ram in the bush' for you. Just trust Him!

Can you think of someone God has brought your way to walk with like that?

Stop and pray for them right now.

Angie and I both agree today that Jesus is our greatest Friend, just as He was to us then. Wow! What a blessing!

We Will Make it

We have the confidence we are believers
We run this race; we are great achievers
We stand together through wind and rain
All kinds of weather, again and again
I know we will make it.

Life has thrown us curve balls
Even though we caught them all
Look at us; we are standing tall
God knew that we could take it.

Every lesson to be learned
Every victory has been earned
Now our life has made this turn
I know we are going to make it.

Together we are standing strong
And with our faith keep holding on
We are the authors of love's great song
Look at us! We made it.

(Philippians 4:13)

Testimony of Encouragement
(We Will Make It)

The Bible declares that a *"threefold cord is hard to be broken"* and also that *"two people are better off than one . . . for if they fall, one will lift up his companion"* (see Ecclesiastes 4:12 and also v.9).

I have never had the experience of being married yet, but my time is coming. I had the opportunity to see my elder daughter experience marriage for the first time in her life; it was hard to hold back the tears. I looked at her standing there saying her vows and was reminded of how God has been my 'husband' through all those years of raising her and her siblings. She was so beautiful standing there with my new son-in-law. That was one of the greatest days of my life and I am sure that it was for her as well.

I have plenty of married couples as friends and have often asked them questions about marriage, to which most reply that marriage is great *work* and that you have to *want* it to work. They have shared with me many of the good things . . . also a lot of concerns — and I have listened.

So many of us single women assume that we will get a "knight in shining armor" riding up in his 'Roze' or Mercedes. Now that well may be the case for some, but it is not reality for most; you may need a lot of patience and polish to make that armor shine, and vice versa. It is important that we get to know whom it is we believe God has brought to us. Always —and I do mean always —involve professional counsel; make sure that they are qualified to help walk you through this area of your life. I am referring to godly counsel, to help guide you in knowing how to identify true love, love that finds you.

Ladies, remember, it is the man who "finds" that "good thing and has favor with the LORD" (see Proverbs 18:22). It is not for us women to go out looking for them [men]. Believe me, when we get busy doing what it is God has called us to do, one day we will look up and there is 'Mr. Right' standing in front of us. Stop trying to look for him!

Oh, and please hear me on this one: keep *you* looking good (men are more physical than we are). Do not wake up rushing to take your child to school . . . stop by the gas station with ashy ankles and wearing penny loafers, sweat pants . . . walk in to pay for your gas right into a buffet line of fine men! Men who, I might add, possibly saw you singing at church before. I can tell you that *that* is one of the most embarrassing moments ever in my life! My 'Mr. Right' could have been one of them. (Don't you dare do that again Terri! — okay, I won't.) And to top it off, that little piece of a car stopped on me and I had to run two miles in those penny loafers to keep from being late for work. Would you just look at that! Sister, please never cheat yourself —always treat yourself.

I have learned since to grease my feet and ankles . . . put on something decent before walking out my door. . . . No, you do not have to tell me twice; once is enough! (*Lol*)

Please wait for God to show you who, what, when, how and where . . . I promise, you will never ever go wrong with Him.

Here is just a little note to you who want to stay single —more power to you, Sister! — enjoy yourself! As for me, I will have 'Mr. Right' on my arm, thank you.

Strengthen Me

What is there to say when you have nothing to say?

How can you even speak when the pain gets in the way?

Anxious to win when you do not even have the fight;
Struck from within, attacking your courage and might.
This, my prayer to my God and my King
Who never fails in anything:
Lift me, O Lord, my Rock, my Hope,
Strengthen my heart, for only You know
The courage I need to make it through the fight.
All my cares are upon You, Lord, tonight!

(Psalm 121)

Testimony of Encouragement
(Strengthen Me)

It was very challenging the day I received a phone call from my cousin who was visiting her mother in my hometown. She startled me when she told me that she had to intervene in my son's plans to take his life. My heart sank; the hurt felt so bad! I have to admit that for a moment all of the Word that I knew left my mind. Suddenly everything around me grew silent . . . it was hard to even talk. It is amazing how you may think that everything is going well when a shock like that comes at you and in those moments, the only thing you can say is 'Jesus'!

I listened to her speak to me as the tears filled my eyes. My chest felt like tons of weight resting on it; my mind was every bit blurred, and just as heavy. Thinking what went wrong; what did I not do or say to my baby? I thought that teaching him the Word of God would comfort him. Then it hit me: What is right about all of this—that my seed would see such a great attack? My cousin began reminding me of what the Word said about my son and together we declared God's Word over him. In desperate times, it is so important to have someone who can pull you back into the peace of God.

We both declared victory until we felt victorious ourselves. We fought back with the greatest weapon, the Word of God. That is why it is so important to study to show ourselves approved; what comes out of you will pull down every stronghold that has come against you and your seed.

I know that it would have been tough for me if God had not sent her. He sent her to that city at the very time my son was contemplating taking his life. Thank You, Jesus! She and her husband love the Lord; and they spoke volumes to me that day, reminding me that we as children of God are daily loaded with benefits. I wept so much during that phone call that my eyes closed up from puffiness, but my ears remained open. (I needed to *hear* what they were speaking.) God revealed to me that the prayers of the righteous make a great difference, and that He always keeps His promises.

Since then my son and I communicate more often. I asked him to contact me at least once a week. I know that this is helping a mother or father out there who may have done your best. Do not give up! Stay with them in this race; keep speaking life to them. Hold on, help is on the way. I tell my son how much I love him and how I am proud of him. Moreover, I am often declaring God's Word over him—that he will know that there are mighty works for him in this earth and no devil in hell will steal that away from him. Did you hear me? No devil will steal them away!

Keep moving forward, Baby.

I Need a Word from You

I need a word from You,
One so pure and true;
A word to free my soul,
A word to let me know
That I am not alone out here on my own.

Wow! Lord, I don't know what to say,
The day You took my breath away . . .
My feeble knees have strength,
Your Word from heaven sent.

You spoke the Word of faith.
I'm strong and not afraid;
I can touch the sky.
Your Word, it makes me fly!

Yes, Lord, I do believe . . .
You make my spirit free.
And Lord, You capture me —
Just by Your Word!

(Psalm 20)

Testimony of Encouragement
(I Need a Word from You)

Have you ever needed God Himself to say something to you, to make sure you knew you were alive? I mean 'something' to help you make it to the next place of ministry in Him. I know I have . . . during times when I felt like a zombie, lost and bewildered. This is a harsh bunch of words but they truly express how I felt.

For some time now, I have walked this earth just existing, not living. I did not really know where to go next or what to do with my life. I needed to know that God had a reason for me to be here still. Guess what! — As always, God reminded me that I was His own, that He had not forgotten.

I remember it so clearly as if it just happened: I was lying on my living room sofa, gazing at the ceiling and questioning whether, or not, I would be something in life. Then I heard it —a voice like the wind whispering softly, "I love you." "Oh, my goodness!" came out of my mouth, and then I began 'balling' like a newborn baby, because I could not believe I had heard the Lord and felt His very Presence in that room . . . . Then to top it off, He said it again! This time I answered, "I know, Lord."

To *hear* God is something I cannot even find words to describe. It was the warmest feeling that I have ever felt up to this day. I have had a few more encounters similar to that along the way and I wish I could have Him speak to me all the time. My goodness, would that not be a treat! The strangest thing is that He did not have to say but just

those few words of comfort, which were more than enough to get me up again and back in the race.

Has God ever spoken to you like that?

Remember, the more time you spend with Him, the more you get to learn about and know Him. The Word of God is true: *"Draw near to God, and He will draw near to you. Cleanse your hands, you sinners; and purify your hearts, you double-minded"* (James 4:8 NKJV).

Down in the Dumps: Whom to Blame?

Have you ever lost it all?
Remember when you stood so tall
And how your back was against the wall
You thought about what made you fall.
And over and over you recalled . . .

(Blame)
What was I supposed to do?
Lord, I did not think of You.
I showed up at church a time or two
And I didn't ask You in.

Right now, I stand here alone
Thinking about how this went wrong.
I can hear that same ole song
That Jesus is my friend.

Was He there when I fell down —
When my face was to the ground
Is He anywhere around?

YES, until the end.

I know you are hurting . . . I am, too!
So many nights I called to you.
Each time I tried, I could not get through
Because you were so busy then;
I kept trying anyway.

Now that I have your full attention,
There is one thing that I should mention:
You no longer have to live in sin,
My life I freely gave.

The future for you is greater than this . . .

Change Your Clothes

Eternal life I do not want you to miss.
T'was Judas that gave the final kiss,
So please, do not turn away,
Come back to Me,
Your life I died to save.

(Isaiah 59:1)

Testimony of Encouragement
(Down in the Dumps: Whom to Blame?)

Hello there, my friend, this is a word for you from God Himself. Isaiah 60:1:

> Arise, shine, for your light has come, and the glory of the LORD rises upon you. See, darkness covers the earth and thick darkness the peoples, but the LORD rises upon you and his glory appears over you.

If you feel down in the dumps, get up from there right now! You have so much to do, so many places to go, and people who really need you. Yes, I said 'really need you.' You are valuable to God. Remember what we talked about earlier: You are mighty — fearfully and wonderfully made (re-read Psalm 139). Did you know that there are people waiting to hear your testimony? They need to hear how you got up and made it work so that they might be encouraged to make it, too. You are reading this book because I made the choice to try.... Yes, I got up! How do you think I made it this far and am still making it day by day? Because another decided to press on, got up and shared their story with me; how that God saved them and helped them to get to their next day.

Our heavenly Father loves you and desires to use you for His kingdom purposes. God is not looking at what you lost, or for that matter, what you gained; God is looking at your heart. So where is your heart? First, have you given your heart to God? Do you know Jesus Christ?

Consider this: What man thinks is totally different from what God thinks. The Bible says that God's ways and thoughts are higher than ours' (see Isaiah 55:8-9). Our heavenly Father determined to save us whatever the cost; and the evidence of this truth is what was finished at Calvary. Yes, sometimes that means moving all of the distractions out of our way to get our attention.

Is it God's wish or will that we fall? Absolutely not! Ecclesiastes 9:11, 12 reveal that *"time and chance happen to them all."* Let us recall Ecclesiastes 3:11-13:

> He hath made everything beautiful in his time: also he hath set the world in their heart, so that no man can find out the work that God maketh from the beginning to the end. I know that there is no good in them, but for a man to rejoice, and to do good in his life. And also that every man should eat and drink, and enjoy the good of all his labour, it is the gift of God.

Remember also Jeremiah 29:11: *"For I know the thoughts that I think toward you, saith the Lord, thoughts of peace, and not of evil, to give you an expected end."* These Scriptures reiterate the truth that God wants good for us, and not evil. (Selah)

Think about and meditate on that for a minute.

How many times has God tried to get through to us before that fall, or that loss? Let us be real . . . and stop trying to cast blame elsewhere. Maybe you have truly been faithful in doing what He has called you to do and still you see no manifestation —been there, done that, and won that trophy! Now for those of you who do fit this category, has there ever been a time when you were watching television, heard an emergency siren, saw these words flash across the screen while a voice announced, 'This is only a test'? All of that was to make sure you (and I) were prepared for the real thing. Could that possibly be what God is doing here?

God's 'emergency system' is His Word; the siren is the Holy Spirit leading you, and the test is you walking this out with Him in charge. Your victory is a very sweet one and your reward is great, all because you were prepared. On top of it all, you will remember that it was God, and only God who brought you through. That is where true worship comes forth; that is where God is pleased. Deuteronomy 29:5, 6 shows us that God is the One who keeps us from harm:

> *And I have led you forty years in the wilderness. Your clothes have not worn out on you, and your sandals have not worn out on your feet. You have not eaten bread, nor have you drunk wine or similar drink, that you may know that I am the LORD your God* (NKJV).

IT IS GOD!

Romans 8:28 tells us ". . . *all things work together for the good of those who love God."* Whatever it is that you feel you just cannot get over or get through, know this: You can, and you will.

There was a time when I thought I would never get over my anger with my children's fathers. Yes, I said 'fathers'—plural. (Okay, don't 'act'!) I cried all the time because I felt they should have been there; by all rights, being fathers, they could have helped in some way. However, I could not . . . did not . . . will not let that history stop me in any way, and neither can you allow your history or present day obstacles to stop you. Oh yes, let me say it again, you cannot let it, or them, or whatever, stop you!

That was my past and because *we* are now in a **new** day, it was your past, too. I am so thankful for the blood of Jesus. Aren't you!

Today I can say that I honestly pray for them, my children's fathers. I ask God to bless their new families. Was it hard sometimes? You had better believe it was . . . my flesh would love to have held them guilty of abandonment, of not being there. Every day, I surrender my life to *the* Father and now it is easier for me to give thanks for them, and for where I am than to become, or to remain bitter.

I encourage you to do as our brother, Apostle Paul, instructed us: *"Lay aside every weight, and the sin"* that keeps you from moving forward (see Hebrews 12:1). I did just that. . . . It is a constant thing and every day gets progressively better. Listen, I, too, was unsure of a great amount of things when I started out, but I kept praying. I kept moving. I kept seeking and asking. Then you know what? One day I realized the more I listened to God in my quiet time and heard Him speaking through my pastor, the more I prayed; and the more I moved in what I heard, the more I progressed.

Yes, I did say that! Let me repeat it in case you did not hear me clearly before. The MORE I LISTENED TO MY PASTOR (the one whom God called to lead, whom God Himself anointed (not we ourselves) to instruct us in the Word, the one whom God called to cover our families (as Moses did the children of Israel), to pray for us when we have challenges getting it right), the more I grew. Do you not know that we need a covering? That is why God ordained and sent His pastors or 'shepherds.' They are here to help us understand better how to live, move, and have our being in this earth. It is our responsibility to study and to stand on God's Word as they lead. When you show up at a worship service to hear what God is saying through him or her, your spirit should agree with and connect with what he or she speaks.

Please understand that it is imperative to be in a Spirit-led church, not only to receive but also to give. Someone is waiting for you; do not give up!

I must share this with you before I move on: I was a member of a small church here in Georgia, and on a particular Sunday, the Pastor encouraged the congregation to hug one another. A certain young woman who had come to visit a couple of times before was present and, upon that instruction, she and I began hugging. I felt the Spirit really drawing me to her; so you know I hugged her, don't you? As I hugged her, she began weeping like nothing I had ever seen before. Later, she confided that it was the first time *ever* that she '*was hugged* and *felt loved*' in her life! She had never before received love as she did that day with that hug . . . she went on to say it felt as if God Himself hugged her. Guess what! She joined the church. Wow! God is so good; He knows what to do, and when to do. Can you believe it . . . she joined because of a loving hug! Thank You, Jesus, for using me. You know, I believe that the Lord did hug her through me. God uses us to share His love with others who so badly need it.

I would have missed that one occasion and many other times if I had given up on life. God's grace allowed me to experience and to see why He created me. You, too, are that person whom God wants to use.

When she told me what my hug had done for her, my heart melted . . . and I could feel God smiling at me. Just think, I had wanted to kill myself a short while back . . . Oh, I must put a praise right there!

Hear me! This is not the time for you to check out or hide in your little room (or big room, which ever fits); these are the best moments of your life. There is an old saying, "When the going gets tough, the tough gets going." God created you in His image and for His glory; now get up and get on your 'good foot' (smile) —someone is waiting just for *you* to come along. Please, do not miss it!

Where My Help Comes From

Just when I was about to
I heard You call to me
Reminding me of Your word spoken over me
To me, through me, about me
I have hope again

The days and nights I lay there
Wondering why
Searching for answers to questions that I . . .
And there you go again
Loving me — Looking into me

Amazing how you know me so well
Saying this too shall pass because you slew my past
I don't have to look back
You took the keys from Hell

I no longer dwell there because I know you care for me
You love me
My mind is made up
And I am free

I will forever look up and stand up
Up is where my help comes from!

(Psalm 121)

Testimony of Encouragement
(Where My Help Comes From)

Man, do I not think about all of the times the Father has come to my rescue! God is such a loving and wonderful Friend. I do not know how I could have survived without Him in my life. Have you ever felt that way? The unfortunate part of being human is that we will have troubles; all kinds of distractions will arise in our lifetime (see Ecclesiastes 9:12). The question is how will we respond?

The fortunate part of that is that those who know Christ have a great advantage over all distractions, for they have His Word. HE is our Help. I am not saying that God does not care for those who have not accepted Him [Jesus]; that would be lying, for the Bible tells us that all souls belong to God (see Ezekiel 18:4). First Corinthians 2:4 explains why it is so important to know God and to have a relationship with Him; otherwise, living here is truly meaningless, selfish and foolish. Life for me before Christ was meaningless and this may be so for you today.

I did not have Christ as my personal Savior in my earlier years; as I said before I knew *of* Him but did not *know* Him. I know now it was *grace* covering me all of those years and His grace has covered you, too. How well I remember the moment of salvation when I accepted Christ into my life at age fourteen, in Long Beach, California. It happened on Long Beach Boulevard and 69th Street at a small storefront Apostolic Church. I never will forget it!

I mentioned in this work that my immediate family was not committed to going to church, so when we moved away from Long Beach, I lost both a wonderful church home and hope. From that moment on, I became very distracted —no church, no Word, and no prayer. Instead, home was a gang-related neighborhood where low-income welfare recipients were as thick as roaches! We were one of them, moving from community to community.

One particular morning I remember walking to school (in Los Angeles) around 6:30 a.m. for what normally was a two-mile walk, or less. I had to get to school by 8:00 a.m. and, according to my mother, I had "better be there on time, or else!" There was this certain man in our neighborhood who would watch me from a distance, one of many fellows that hung out there. Well, do you know that this 'brotha' jumped out from behind a building in front of me that morning! Although I tried not to show it, I was terrified and paralyzed. He told me that he was "going to get me" one day. (I am putting this very mildly because the words he used are not suitable for readers.) I did not know what to do because I was too far away from home to run back . . . and had to be at school for a special project in our music class. I mustered enough courage to tell the guy that he was cute and that he could come by my house later. He finally let me pass by. That was the creepiest moment of my life. I did tell my mom and my boyfriend, at that time (my oldest child's father). As you can imagine, my emotions were flying everywhere!

A few days later, that person came to my front door and asked for me. Of course, I would not go to the door. My sister closed the door on him and we sat back down . . . then a few minutes later in came a big shopping cart through our large glass window; that scared the 'holy heaven' out of me and my family! My boyfriend chased down that fellow and almost killed him that day! I never dealt with that issue after then . . . but once again, I had to move, and this time with a baby inside my womb at the age of 16.

I lived with friends off and on, here and there, which was a hot sticky mess —I hated life. I continued attending school until they found out that I was pregnant; then I enrolled in an alternative school —one where pregnant girls fought each other. Oh, what a mess I was in then! I asked God where my help was through all of this . . . He was right there. I just could not *see* Him at work.

I gave up on everything and walked into an abortion clinic. As I lay there, the doctor told me I needed to get to a hospital because I was dilating; she wanted to call for an ambulance but I would not allow it. Can you imagine! Believe it, or not, God was working then, and you will see how in just a minute.

The pain was so bad; I just wanted all the hurt to go away, and I tried everything in my power to end it. Well, I did have my little angel, who weighed in at 6lbs., 15 ounces.

Oh, I feel I am helping someone right here to just "Let go, and let God."

God saved one of the greatest blessings of my life that day, my eldest child. I cannot even begin to tell you how much she has brought joy to me, as well as to so many that have crossed her path. She is a loving daughter, sister, wife, and mother —a very giving and mighty woman in Christ who blesses me over, and over again. This same child has taken care of all of her siblings' needs whenever needed and has provided for me during my hardest years. God has done the same for me through my two youngest ones.

Can you see God's hand at work?

He will keep you when you do not know how to keep yourself, and I did not know how to keep myself. I was afraid . . . experienced all kinds of anxieties . . . extremely stressed out and feeling guilty of being too young to have children. All of these things were swarming my mind.

Listen, you do not have to live life that way: God has the perfect plan for your life; just trust Him. He was there to help me when I did not know how to help myself. I could not see it then but God was there on my way to school that morning, for what kept that man from dragging me into any one of those abandoned apartments when he could have so easily done so? God —it was God! Please let me put a praise right there. Thank You, Jesus! When I think about all the Lord has brought me out of and through, my soul screams 'Hallelujah!'

I must admit that I have encountered many other challenges since that moment, things that I will share later. However, today, know that I *know* God for myself that my *Help* arrived when I needed Him. He is right there whenever I call, and even when I fail to do so. Aren't you thankful to have a Friend in God, Who comes when we need Him and even when we do not realize we do? I am. "Where does my help come from?" It comes from God. For you reading this now, know that God is always there and all you have to do is call on Him; He will answer. He heals, He saves, and He surely delivers.

The Lord

The Lord shepherds me, covers me,
    Encourages me with just a word;

The Lord guides me, provides for me,
    Touches me with His love;

The Lord calls me, holds on to me,
    Blesses me with amazing joy;

The Lord heals me, prays for me, comforts me,
    Ministers to me where I am;

The Lord teaches me, gives peace to me,
    Saves me from dangers unseen;

The Lord changes me, cleanses me,
    Prepares me for the journey ahead;

The Lord sings over me, strengthens me,
    He is my daily bread.

(Psalm 23)

Testimony of Encouragement
(The LORD)

It is hard to stop when you are talking about such a great King. A matter of fact, He is the greatest! I can go on and on praising God; there is just so much to say about Him, His mercies do endure forever. Is it not amazing how much God loves us? Oh, how He loves us! Can you not feel His love? I can. I do not believe we can fully understand how much He desires for us to be well and blessed.

One of my colleagues, a sister-in-Christ, is always saying that because God is our Father, we are 'smothered, covered, and chunked.' I laughed so hard when I heard it because I knew what she was talking about . . . still get a little tickled hearing her say it now. You know, she is right: God does have us covered!

If you have ever spent time here in the South, especially in Atlanta, you may have noticed that almost every other corner has a Waffle House restaurant. At least once a month, I stop in . . . to me breakfast there is the best. I'll listen to the waitress and observe how, after taking food orders, she begins 'barking' them out to the head cook who sometimes repeats it or may simply choose to place certain items on a platter to note special requests (Yes, my mouth is watering right now, too!). Minutes later the meal is set before you looking and smelling extraordinarily good, for which you are thankful. You also give thanks that the cook showed up!

God wants us to understand how extraordinary we are. He wants us to know the truth and to live extraordinary lives. The Father's love for us is so great and awesome that He sent Jesus to live, die, and then rise again, so that we, too, might live —live abundantly! Think about that! I am so happy to know how much I am loved —that GOD made sure I was born; even more that I would live and live a life of abundance, a healthy, wealthy, prosperous, joyous life in worship of Him and fellowship with others. JESUS is our Life, our Friend, Comforter, and Helper. God is so good! Don't you agree? Go ahead, stop right here and praise God —you know you want to!

He Will Use . . .

HE will use your hands to hug someone unloved

HE will use your feet to go into the slums

HE will use your mouth for His words to speak

HE will use your trials to make a life complete

HE will use your life for the world to display

Spread the *Good News* to change someone today

HE will use your mother's testimonies of old

HE will use your father's victories untold

Your sister HE may choose to speak into your life

If HE can use the donkey, HE can choose just whom HE likes

Your brother may be a bother but HE may use him, too

To keep you on your knees so often, HE will do.

HE will use you!

(I Peter 4:10)

Testimony of Encouragement
(He Will Use)

As a young girl, all I wanted to do was to grow up and sing like 'The Emotions' or Ms. Natalie Cole. Ours was not a God-centered home; we knew about Jesus but we did not serve Him in our daily walk. My sister and I went to church whenever our aunts could come get us and take us there. Oh, how thankful I am for them! How amazing it is that God sets people in your path to cover you when you do not even know how to cover yourself — thank You, J E S U S! (Selah)

My two close friends and I dreamt of being big stars when we were little girls. We even put long sheets on our heads pretending it was hair, and sang to The Emotions' soundtrack in front of a mirror. Although they did not need to adorn their heads with sheets but probably did so to keep me from feeling out of place, I needed to wear those sheets because my head was a hot, nappy mess!

Those early childhood dreams slowly faded as we grew up and each of us relocated to different places, becoming parents ourselves. I stay in contact with one of the women as much as I can, for in one way or another we have touched each other's life. Each of us has gone through some kind of major trial or test through the years.

Today, I am 'saved, sanctified —filled with the Holy Ghost'! (Ya'll know what I mean.) I have witnessed God's reaching out to hurting people through ministry —even as much as a hug. God can use any situation or circumstance in your life to bring Him glory, just as He has done for my two friends and me. I grew up living on food stamps through most of my childhood, and frequenting the Welfare Office as a teenage mom, myself. Yes, we faced a lot of hard times growing up —but God! Do you not know that God will wipe that pain away through a word, or a smile?

I often think back on the joy we shared pretending then . . . . Pretense made me forget we were poor —plus we had so much fun together! Those moments I have never forgotten, and they make me smile even now.

Reflect for a moment on how God has used you, or think about how He may use you to touch someone, to leave a lasting impression of His Spirit in another's life. Okay now, if you are taking too long to think about it, we might have a problem! (Smile)

In Matthew 28:20 Jesus told His disciples to go into the world and preach the *Good News*. It is by the Spirit of Christ that we *go* . . . . Maybe now is the time for a refreshing in the Spirit, time for us to be fully open to the Spirit of God, the *Holy Spirit*. He is that Perfect Gentleman, waiting for you to invite Him to enter . . . and you can get up and ask Him to renew you right now —yes, right now!

As a single woman, I often think about that special someone opening the door for me, about the joy of a nice conversation or a pleasant night out. Well, our God is more than that —HE is amazing! There have been times when I have sat silently in the pew at church and cried when I thought on God and His compassion and mercy towards us; it left me speechless.

God wants to use us. And when you say, "I want to be used by God," you had better mean it! It takes courage to say that. When you say "God, use me," look out! —He will. Most of the time it is not going to be as you expect or think.

The old saying, "Be careful what you ask for because you just might get it" rings so true. Make sure that what you are asking for from God you are prepared to handle, and all that comes with it. God knows what this world needs and He knows what is best for us and for others.

Many times God has used my sister to speak words that have touched my soul; she did not know what I was facing at that time, but I knew . . . additionally, I knew it was God letting me know that He was listening to me, to my prayers. God can use anyone to get His point across, whether it is you or another to whom He is trying to communicate. WOW! Is that not a wonderful thing?

God will go to great lengths to make sure we understand how much He cares . . . . His purpose is already complete and His will is to get us to our destiny. I am happy He wants to make sure that we all are all right —aren't you?

Mighty

Oh, so mighty you are —

So strong and standing tall,
Ruler of generations,
Strength is your determination.

Reaching your destination,
Your mind is the key
For where you are to be:
Faint echoes of voices
Calling and crying out
To leaders of this future,
Making the silence shout,
Defeating fear with victory,
Conquering every war,
Making your mark in history,
Mighty, so mighty you are!

Stand on that solid ground,
The force is strong behind you,
Never again backing down,
You are where you want to be – where you should be.
Mighty you are!

(Jeremiah 1:7-10)

Testimony of Encouragement
(Mighty)

"Keep on Trucking" was a song heard back in the day. Yet, back in the day, I used to sit back and think that God was supposed to bring everything to me. "Where is my silver platter?" was my mindset. Now I can just visualize God saying, "Yes, where is it?" (*Lol*)

There was never a try in my spirit at all; I waited around day after day, wasting time, sitting back watching television, cleaning the house over, and over, singing in the mirror, hanging in with the same posse —NO PLANS AT ALL! (Does it sound familiar?) **Time** was passing me by and all I would do was cry because I did not see anything coming together for me. (Oh, somebody out there can feel me right now!) If I were to get where I was supposed to be in life, I believed that God was the One to do it; after all, He created me. OMG! How ridiculous! True, God created us, and wonderfully at that, for we have so many special gifts and talents; the problem is that I was not praying or planning to use what God has given me.

How much time have you wasted, day in and day out, talking about what you want to do instead of just doing it? Faith requires action. Habakkuk 2:2 tells us to *"Write the vision and make it plain . . . ."* We (my posse and I) were not the only ones not taking action; there are so many out here today still doing the same thing and thinking the same way. Does that not sound scary! That should tell you something: Change your way of thinking — COME OUT OF THAT THINKING! RIGHT NOW!

Fear not! Change your thoughts. There is one thing that I have learned about **FEAR** or *False Evidence Appearing Real:* It is a scam from the pit of hell, used to stop God's people from living a Kingdom life! This small word has effectively paralyzed many souls, including me at one point. Well, enough is enough! It is long overdue that we take authority over every thought that exalts itself against the knowledge of God and His Word, and we must do so in action and with power. That power is in our tongue. Let the words of your mouth speak life, my friend. Speak life over yourself and your family, your ministry, your gifts and talents. Speak LIFE!

Let me remind you of who you are. You are mighty! God created you and me in His image, to rule and to have dominion in the earth (read Genesis 1:27). The challenge is that this world has distracted so many from the road to destiny. The blessing is that we already have the power to rule, power given to us through Jesus Christ our Lord and Savior, over 2000 years ago. The enemy (Satan) has used distractions and attacks to keep us from our potential, but do not be fooled, for what the enemy stole from us in Eden we re-gained in greater capacity through the cross —Jesus' death, burial, and, most definitely, His resurrection! AMEN. Can *we* put a praise right there? Go ahead; I will wait.

It is our right to live victoriously; it is our right to walk in victory after victory, and it is our right to possess the land. We do not have to lie down and take what Satan is dishing out . . . and we will not stay in a position of never enough when we have the opportunity of being and receiving more. I am not talking about material possessions only, so do not get it twisted. Yes, they are a part of what God wants to give to us; however, they come when we do what we are supposed to do *first*. Meditate on Matthew 6:33: *"But seek first the kingdom of God and His righteousness, and all these things shall be added to you"* (NKJV).

There are so many lives depending on you and me to live out divine destiny. Lives of people will be touched on our journey and at our journey's peak when we decide to live out our individual purpose in the earth. Hearts will be encouraged; minds renewed, and generations charged up because we chose to rise to the occasion and decided not to accept less than God's perfect plans and thoughts . . . .

The Word of God says, *". . . since we are surrounded by such a great cloud of witnesses, let us throw off everything that hinders and the sin that so easily entangles"* (Hebrews 12:1 NIV). Remember always to walk by faith and not by sight. Furthermore, according to Philippians 3:14: Let us *"press toward the mark for the prize of the high calling of God in Christ Jesus."* Our spiritual father declared to us that the millionaire is within; it is not about the money but the ideas you (we) are holding inside of us. WOW! That blew my mind! I declare that I am mighty enough to be victorious.

How about you?

What I Treasure Most

What I treasure most are the moments I open my eyes
See a new dawning and the beautiful sunrise
What I treasure most are the moments I make my bed
Standing on my feet and brushing my own head
What I treasure most are the times I dial my phone
Calling up a loved one and finding them at home
What I treasure most is laughter I hear each night
Voices of my children — echoing so bright
What I treasure most is the love that we both share
My heavenly Father and I — and this I do declare
Because of His tender love, I have such wonderful things
Unforgettable, precious moments, only He can bring
What I treasure most may not matter much to you
Yet every moment is precious, so consider what you do.

(Matthew 6:25- 34)

Testimony of Encouragement
(*What I Treasure Most*)

I received a phone call from a loved one who told me that her daughter had passed away from cancer. My heart hurt. Not only did I hurt for her, but I also hurt because I did not get (had not gone) to tell the deceased that I loved her (before she died). Oh, I had the chance to write her a letter, but never did. Her passing left me with regrets. I told my loved one that I was so sorry, and how I regretted not having kept in touch as much as I could have. Then I asked for her forgiveness, and she forgave me.

I wonder if there is someone in your life or, for that matter, out of your life, that you know you should be talking to or helping right now. God has put them on your heart more than a time or two and you still keep ignoring it —DON'T! It could end up much too late! Hold on to those moments; embrace where you are, stop complaining about crazy things. It does no good, anyway.

"To love *and* forgive" is a phrase that hits hard for many people, especially me. I was angry with my mother for past situations that occurred in our lives. I felt so bitter because my life was so 'jacked up' and I did not know how or if I could ever straighten it out. The challenge was *me*— Mother was moving on with living while *I* held on to the past. I asked God, 'What was the deal?' The deal was she understood the principle of forgiveness; she knew God had forgiven her, and so she moved on.

I, on the other hand, wanted to keep hate alive by staying angry — I was comfortable that way. I falsely believed that I had control over her by holding her guilty of what Jesus had forgiven her. Actually, I was denying my own freedom, because I did not want to move on until I saw her hurting, as I was hurting. Was that evil or what? Yet it is the truth.

Finally, I moved forward and asked my mom for forgiveness of my selfish ways. She forgave me, and today we love each other more than ever. I realize that I only have one mother and I want to take advantage of the time we have together here on this earth. I will never allow my thoughts and attitude to get that way about anyone else again. My controlling thought now is that we only have one life, so we are going to live it well.

Take a moment out of your day to tell a family member or loved one that you really love them. Bake a cake for someone you know. Send a 'thank-you note' to a co-worker just for smiling at you. Pay for someone's lunch or pay a bill. Most importantly, do not forget to love yourself!

I really try to enjoy the times I have with my children when we sit together and talk. We share not only the Word of God; we catch up on what is going on in their lives. One thing that I often hear my spiritual father talk about is families not sitting and eating together anymore; it is sadly true. This world has so many of us distracted until the most important things do not matter anymore. Well, it is time to get back to the basics: God should be first, and then family, followed by ministry. You should deliberately plan more time with your family; I promise you that it will be worth every minute. Every moment in life is so precious; be mindful of how you spend yours. Additionally, let us pray one for another!

If You Love Me

You held onto me too tight . . .
It wasn't supposed to be forever.
What will you do with your life now that we are apart?
Have you made plans?
Do you have dreams of your own?

Do you have goals?
Or do you even know?
Have you put your life into this one little bottle?
Open it up now, do that for me.
Go on and live again!
Don't stop, because time hasn't, and it won't.
Take a look around,
Get up and go out for a walk.
Breathe in and breathe out,
Sit down with someone and talk.
Look in that mirror and say to yourself:
If you love me,
You will go out and live again.

(Romans 13:10)

Testimony of Encouragement
(If You Love Me)

Sometimes it is hard to let go of those we love and the things we love the most. I recently took my youngest to Ohio for her first year of college. The moment for me was 'bitter-sweet.' I cannot say the same for her, because she had the biggest 'chess cat' grin on her face as we drove onto that campus. I was not sure if that smile was because she was happy for a new beginning, or happier about that day being the last day she and Mom would be together. Humm, either way, I was a proud momma!

As I drove off the campus, tears rolled down my face, tears I had held back earlier because I wanted this to be a wonderful day for her. They flowed when I realized that this was it; there was no one left to tell what to do . . . just me. All excuses were now out the window! My overused excuse of putting my 'life on the back burner for my children' was over. Now, I had no other choice but to do it.

Do you feel that way, too?

I encourage you to take a deep breath and jump right on into deep water because if you do not, I assure you there will be regrets. Stop wasting time! We are not getting any younger and time waits for no one. Just get out there and get into the flow of things, because *"God has not given us a spirit of fear, but of power and of love and of a sound mind"* (2 Timothy 1:7).

My offspring are very strong-willed children; they forced me to let go. "What do I mean?" Whenever I became too overwhelming, they were not afraid to let me know it. I honored them by learning to give them their space, which was not always easy being a single parent. You carry so much responsibility; you have to be both parents at once. How does one manage that? (Somebody out there knows exactly what I am talking about.) I have done it —the single parenting —for over twenty-eight years. Having reared three children, my answer to the question "How?" is always, 'It was Jesus and me.'

Breaking those old, ugly habits of single parenting can be quite challenging but certainly obtainable. I know because I tried holding on to the parenting role by nurturing my sister's children. Although we knew they needed direction, which was her responsibility and not mine, I got caught up in it. Call it a habit, if you will . . . I just felt *I* had to look after them. Then God began showing me how that was so distracting, for at the time, I could not see what He wanted for me. Let me say this (which I have heard said more than once), 'Where God is taking you some cannot go.' Yes, there are ties that need cutting and sometimes the cutting hurts, but still the cutting must come, or all will suffer. Many of us as single parents rear our children and because we are sometimes unsure of where God is taking us or we fear the unknown, we slip back into old patterns of living. Do not do that!

To avoid any misunderstanding, certainly, some do have to take on the responsibility of parenting because of some unfortunate event in life; you have decided to make a difference in the lives of the children affected. Additionally, there are those champions among us who have taken it upon themselves to adopt or foster a child —much love to you! You are my heroes and "she roes."

But to you who know that God has been calling you up to something greater and you have fallen into that 'parenting trap,' knowing that you are supposed to be doing something else —stop! That is not your responsibility at this time; you are allowing distractions and you will end up traveling a road to nowhere. It is time to get going and NOW is the time!

To let you know how things are going, I have penned this first book and another is on the way. I speak with God daily . . . and give Him thanks for His thoughts and plans to me. I am planning and eating better, managing my time better, and learning to let go of what *was,* and to live for what *is* to come. Will you please live, too? Amen.

Am I Really Trying?

I'm trying to let go
I'm trying to get out
I'm trying to do better
I'm trying not to doubt.

I'm trying not to answer
I'm trying not to call
I'm trying to be on time
I'm trying not to fall.

I'm trying not to cheat
I'm trying not to yell
I'm trying to believe
I'm trying not to tell.

I'm trying to have hope
I'm trying hard to win
I'm trying to say no
I'm trying not to sin.

Trying . . . Am I really?

(Philippians 3:14)

Testimony of Encouragement
(Am I Really Trying?)

I believe the Word says it best — *"lay aside every weight and the sin that so easily besets us . . ."* (cf. Hebrews 12:1a).

My friend, what is it that has you captured? Please do not say that it is *love* when you know that *peace* has been far from that relationship, especially that relationship with God. How long? Yes, I put it out there; how long are you going to stay entangled? It is time to get your life back.

I know what it feels like to keep going around that same old mountain, again, and again, until you wake up one morning and your hair is grey. And for what? Let us stop that, okay! My mother often said that when you start something go ahead and finish it. So just touching the surface is not going to help get you free; you must decide that you are going to do it, and then just do it!

All effort is good and there is nothing wrong with trying, so please do not misunderstand me . . . nevertheless, there is still another saying that "If at first you don't ...." Okay, you finish the rest. The challenge is when 'trying' becomes the excuse. You know when you have not given it your best . . . we all know when 99.9% does not measure up.

The Bible tells us that God searches the heart of man. God definitely knows when we are giving our best and He will hold us accountable. It is up to us. Sometimes the greatest challenge is getting us to realize that with God all things are possible. We must remember that we have already overcome by Jesus' blood and the word of our testimony. If there is a challenge that seems too great, lean on God . . . It is by His power and His might. God knows the end from the beginning of time . . . God knows all.

When you allow God to walk with you through it all, you cannot — you will not go wrong. God will show you how to have good success. Involving the Lord from the beginning will save you a lot of drama and precious time. Time we do not want to keep wasting!

Be Glad in it

What a beautiful day this is!
The sun is breaking through.
Even with a cloudy sky,
It was created just for you:

The morning birds are singing;
Listen to the sound,
The melody of peace
Is ringing all around,

Inviting you to come in it
And step into your place,
To feel the morning breeze
And the dew upon your face.

Although but for a moment
When this day will take its end,
The beauty for the morning
Is that it will come again.

(Psalm 118:24)

Testimony of Encouragement
(Be Glad In It)

It was early — 5:00 in the morning —and I was tired. Dizziness hit me for a moment, having to wake up so early, because I am so not a morning person! It took me another moment to get it together. I have worked nights for a while, so getting into bed early is a real task. Tossing and turning, trying to get to sleep can be bothersome. Has this ever happened to you? —sitting up until you get so sleepy that you can barely carry yourself off to bed. Help us, Lord! Yet, I know things are getting better.

The blessing in falling off to sleep is opening up one's eyes into a brand new day God has given. I am especially thankful to wake up to birds singing outside of my window. Leaving my window open at night would be fine, except that I now, seemingly, have become a "snack" to little bugs that climb through the screen. What a wonderful world!

Although a certain day may not feel as great as others . . . know that it is still a *good* day. Remember that everything God made is definitely *good*. Please, do not forget that! Each day brings new mercies, new possibilities, new expectations and new ideas. Each day gives us an opportunity to start over again, and for that, I am most thankful!

Aren't you? Who would not want a clean slate?

You may be waking up to face some of the most challenging moments of your life. It does not matter what it looks like. Just take a moment to yourself; sneak away into a corner and begin thanking God for that day . . . thank Him for allowing you even to be in the position you are in at that moment. God knows that you can handle what you are facing, so walk through it. I promise that your perspective will begin to change and you will see more clearly that you are already victorious.

Speaking with a 'sister' at my church one Sunday, I shared how hard it is for me to remain in a depressed state of mind. I believe this comes as a direct result of my professions of God's Word. I profess His joy and His peace. I profess numerous Bible verses over my family and me; this should be the believer's daily routine. I believe that because of these professions, life's perspective will change. Mine definitely has!

Time Waits for No One

Whatever is has already been

And what will be has been before.

A different time of faces and places—

Destiny stands at every door.

Opportunity comes again

To those who choose to want it more.

In the beginning, He created the end,

No heart can fathom what is in store.

So what do we gain in all our labor

If in our hearts, we hold no truth?

Are we the keeper of our brother

Or have we robbed him of his youth?

And so I ask this question:

Are we living or just space we occupy?

For time will wait for no one

And eternity is drawing nigh.

(Ecclesiastes 3:10)

Testimony of Encouragement
(Time Waits for No One)

Time does not wait. The sooner I got that, the better, and the sooner you get it, the better! It is vitally important to keep on moving. "Moving to where?" I am glad you asked. FORWARD! —in the pre-planned direction God has for you and for me.

If you have ever noticed, each day differs from the last. As long as I have been saved,

I have recognized that God has never come at me the same way. Why should we do the same? It is time to stop! After all, we are created in His image. Proverbs 3:5, 6 declares that by trusting in God He directs your path and makes the way straight for you.

There have been many—I do mean *many*—challenging moments on this journey because of my failure to allow God to take the lead. You may be thinking that I should have been stronger and trusted God more. Yes, you are right, but many of us came from the "other side of the track" and have a lot of growing up to do. "Pity-party Terri" is who I was.

I wanted to throw in the towel, washcloth, soap and bathtub —it was ridiculous! Every time a decision came up that was a bit challenging for me, instead of taking it to God, I would go off my emotions or call for advice from a friend —one that I knew I could persuade. That was not cool! Time was still passing by while I was pretending to get it together. How much time must pass before we get it together? Think about all those souls waiting on us to make a decision to change.

Oh, have I learned! I looked at myself and asked, "How long will you stay in this state, girl?" With tears running down my face I declared, "Today is it." At that moment, I became more conscious of letting God in and much more aware of what I was speaking in order to keep from going back again. God's Word tells us to *"Let the words of our mouth and the meditation of our heart be acceptable in Your sight, O Lord..."* (Psalm 19:14). HE is our strength and Redeemer.

Did you know that God's Holy Spirit is such a perfect Gentlemen? He does not, and will not override *our* will. He loves an invitation to fellowship with us; and not only that, He wants to be our Guide to the best places. I know that today. I also know that it was the grace and power of God that kept me from doing some crazy things . . . our 'will' can go a little far left sometimes.

I want to be a blessing to many people but concentrating on my situation all the time was and is a big waste of time. I find that the more time I spend talking to God and giving everything over to Him, the less time I waste doing unproductive things.

How much time have you wasted?

Well, today is another chance to work it out . . . . Are you glad that God has given us this chance to discover new things? If we just allow Him that opportunity, He makes that change for us (my writing this book is evidence). This project was the farthest thing from my mind; and those who know me will tell you that I live, breathe, and eat music; that nothing else mattered as long as I got my music going in my direction.

Well, mainly due to that mindset, I have suffered many 'screw ups.' Now that God and I are in a 'One-on-one,' I am learning how to divide my time between music, writing, family and ministry. We have to have a balance. God will show you that balance; it is up to you to get the ball rolling. There are many things on my mind to do, but I want it to be the right timing. This can be for those who are thinking of moving from one place to another or one career to another: Make sure that God is making that move with you, that it is not you alone.

What is it that you should be doing right now?

We will not waste another moment, will we? We just do not have the time. Do you feel me on this one?

The greatest blessing about managing our time properly is that we then have more of it to use on other things. I tell you that being obedient is better than sacrificing. I said it earlier: Everything depends on your relationship with the Father. God will send people or messages through people . . . . It is up to you to understand when God is ministering to you. If you are having a challenge knowing when fasting and praying may be necessary, receive this awesome weapon that helped me: Talk to your leadership about how to fast and pray for direction, how to hear the voice of God. (Our Bishop teaches us very well on how to fast and pray.) Remember, if you are not sure, always seek guidance from someone who knows the Word and lives the Word of God.

Most importantly, just keep moving!

Birth, Pregnancy, Conception

This situation is very real — I have been trying hard to make it happen.

The seed was planted at my birth. "Why?" I asked. "Why so long?"

So that I wouldn't miscarry came the answer,

And so that I would know it was Him and not me.

This has been a dream and now a vision,

This decision has taken faith to wait, and wait I will until the due date.

While waiting I know what I must do — keep my focus and mind on You,

Oh Lord, looking at You, seeking You,

I didn't have this chance some time ago.

This vision would have been stillborn You knew.

Oh, how I needed to grow!

There would be no victory or gain.

I must admit that sometimes the pain

Causes me to cry out and I want to quit,

But I keep on because of You, and when I think, I grin;

I know the new beginning begins.

I can breathe lighter because I have conceived;
my day for blessings awaits me.

Open doors are there to overtake, to motivate me.

If I choose to move too fast, the end of this moment will not even last.

So I let Patience have her perfect way . . .

In the meantime, I will celebrate your arrival day.

Listen, we cannot miscarry or conceive out of design

Because the vision inside is going to blow your mind!

(Psalm 127:1-3; Psalm 27:14)

Testimony of Encouragement
(Birth, Pregnancy, Conception)

It was hard for me to wait on God. Have you ever been in that place? I went ahead of Him so many times and faced disaster somewhere in the middle, especially with what I call the "3-M syndrome" —money, men and the mind —things I have had to work on for quite some time. Praise God, for mercy and grace!

I had to learn that when we move out of the will of God we forfeit so much, especially time. Life is a process; there is a time and a season for all things. King Solomon wisely taught, *"To everything there is a season and time to every purpose under heaven"* (see Ecclesiastes 3). There will come a time when we will be proven, the end being that we come out like pure gold or silver (see Psalm 66:10) —'beautiful' describes it best. I have come to understand that *process* is so necessary and one's reaction to the process is crucial. In it all, just know that God's blessings are sure.

For over twenty-eight years, I have been a single mom and never married. Whew! It took a lot to release that. Although I have come close [marrying] on a few occasions, I thank God I did not. I was not ready . . . with what was going on in my life, let alone committing to marriage. Many of my actions were so emotional and far from spiritual in nature. "Have I learned?" you ask. Oh, yes! I have dedicated my life to Christ for several years now, and I did say "dedicated" because it is a choice, one I make every day as I arise and ask God to create in me a clean heart and a renewed mind. Everyday Satan is coming at us with all kinds of crazy ideas and thoughts; it is up to us to let him hang around, or to tell that booger to get lost. We have the power and it is time we used it!

My children sat me down to talk to me about being alone. Wow! They had such good suggestions for me, and, as most parents would have done, I allowed them to make their speeches. When it was my turn to respond this was my reply: 'I'm going to hold out, because I know God has a plan for me and I expect Him to come through' (see Jeremiah 29:11). I added, 'Did you hear me? I expect Him to come through.'

What is your reply?

While we wait, it is our responsibility to pursue God, to chase after God. I must confess that I have fallen short in that area on a couple of occasions but I am better now. We must know that our due season will come; as long as we keep God first, we are destined to reap a good harvest. Whether we have invested time, money, or devotion, we will reap what we have planted.

What have you been planting?

"Be not deceived; God is not mocked: for whatsoever a man soweth, THAT shall he also reap" (Galatians 6:7, 8). The Word in verse 8 continues, *"For he that soweth to his flesh shall of the flesh reap corruption, but he that soweth to the Spirit shall of the Spirit reap life everlasting."*

We can look at this verse in two ways: Not only do we get the reward of Heaven forever, but also we can experience what true living really is here on Earth. Don't you think that is worth waiting for? Yes, it is not always easy but it is truly worth it.

Let me share this with you: I have had the opportunity to sing to the glory of God before thousands each week —truly breath taking! Our church members have shared how their lives have changed because of what God is doing through my vessel and that blesses me. I want always to be available for God to use me.

What about you?

"For it is by grace that [we] have been saved, through faith — and that not of ourselves, it is the gift of God . . . ." (Ephesians 2:8).

God has already provided the promises . . . He is waiting on you. It is not about OUR timing —it is about His. It is about OUR GROWING UP! God intends to protect us from crop failure, so that what we have sown can feed the nations.

Thank you, Lord!

Thank you, Lord, for your grace
Thank you, Lord, for this hour
Thank you, Lord, for this place
Thank you, Lord, for your power
Thank you, Lord, for your love
Thank you, Lord, for every answer
Thank you, Lord, for more than enough
Thank you, Lord, for the laughter
Thank you, Lord, for your Glory
Thank you, Lord, for this joy
Thank you, Lord, for your story—
Sharing it with the world
Thank you, Lord!

Testimony of Encouragement
(Thank You, Lord)

Have you ever just stopped to take time out to tell the Lord "Thank You"? There are moments when I just think about God and start crying —He is so wonderful! I am glad that He created me to love Him and live for Him. How about you?

Do you know that our main purpose for being here is to love on God? I have to admit that I repented for all of the times I neglected to give Him praise. He is so beautiful and He is so merciful. You and I know what He has been to us and our families . . . take a moment and let that marinate.

Is He "Alpha and Omega" in your life, or just another thought?

There is so much that we can thank God for . . . just having life is enough already. It is amazing how each day God has something new for us to walk into. This day is not like yesterday and tomorrow will not be like today; they each hold their own treasures.

Can you imagine giving up your child (those of you who have children)? I look at my son and my daughters and just the thought of them being gone is a little frightening. My love is with those of you whose loved ones have gone on before you. Well, God gave up someone He loved so much for you and me, and His name is **Jesus.**

Think about your John, Judy, Katelyn or Keisha having to take on a crucifixion or having to be spit upon, hated, and then to be beaten beyond recognition. I cannot . . . and do not want to think about it, but guess what! —all this did happen and it happened to our Jesus at Calvary.

The reason why we are here is that God did that for us —sacrificed His only Beloved Son! Thank You, Lord Jesus; I am forever grateful! Thank You, Father, for Your love is so great toward us. You are so merciful and loving.

Every time that you think of something God has done, just start thanking Him. Yes, I know; there is just so, so much —isn't it?

A Masterpiece in the Making

Fearfully and wonderful

Already created beautiful
Nothing is comparable
Uniquely designed and suitable
Altered just a little in a sinful empty space
Scratched, bruised and tilted in a lost, empty place
But the Master of design took you up again
Polished you to shine after ridding you of your sin
Cleared away the dross and stain
That life itself attached
The most beautiful masterpiece —
Now what do you think of that!

(Psalm 139:14, 15)

Testimony of Encouragement
(A Masterpiece in the Making)

Years ago, I wrote a piece called "Vessel of Honor." This song was a testament of my birth in Jesus Christ. An earlier testimony included the trials of moving with a man to Atlanta, and then the trauma of being 'put out.' Let me share with you how through that situation I came alive.

Need I say that everything was not always 'peaches-n-crème'? I had my moments, yet I would not change it for anything this world has to offer. This was my beginning of freedom from sin, shame and drama to my new start in a life of hope, peace and joy. This was the beginning of my journey with *Jesus*.

I think back on those days sometimes and see how God moved in those situations to make me the vessel I am today. There were moments when the food supply was so low, bills were overdue, children were acting up, and men wanting to be with me —all of which drew me to my knees in prayer even more and more. Do you know one day I looked up and God had answered them all!

There is absolutely nothing in this entire world too hard for God. You have to grab hold of that —GOD is the only true and living God! I am a living witness of the Lord who testifies to real life experiences, real life challenges, and great outcomes, all because of His grace.

I know that it may seem hard for change to come, but the moment in which you surrender is the very moment that change occurs. In that moment, you become a masterpiece in the making.

Remember that life is a journey that we all are on; the way we respond to where we are going will make all the difference. Amen.

My Love Letter to God

I found out what true love is when I loved You
You took me for what I was and what I was not
God! You loved me anyway
You looked through me like seeing sand in an hourglass
Building me up in so many ways where I was fading fast.

You are my strength and You were my strength when I had nothing left
You surprised me with joy; You loved me through
my hurts and through the pain
And even in the laughter and
Yes, even those disappointing moments that
broke your heart the day after . . .
Even then, You still loved me
You held me and made every moment count
God! You love me so much

Sometimes I am without words because of the way You love me
My heart melts and I cry for joy and happiness all at once
So many lovely things all mixed up together
I am more in love with You than ever

I feel so loved and I am not afraid anymore of love
I am not afraid anymore to love
Because I found out what love is the moment I fell in love
with You, God.

(Psalm 18:1, 2)

Testimony of Encouragement
(My Love Letter to God)

One day in prayer I cried, and cried and cried . . . that was all I could do; I felt so wonderful inside! I tried stopping but could not. I could not even think on anything else but telling God how much I loved Him. My eyes swelled from crying; my face was red and my nose, stuffy . . . those of you who have experienced this know what I am saying. If, perhaps, you have not experienced God in such a way as this, I hope that you do. Amen!

When God comes in and takes over, the room is so full of His sweet presence and you can feel His Spirit hovering so greatly, it is hard to find words to thank Him. All you want to do is love on Him as much as you can. His presence is so magnificent that your whole being is free from every thought; every care is gone. The power in that fellowship is so awesome you may want to run, or even bow down on your knees with your face to the floor. Sometimes, I sit or pace the floor, my hands lifted high, praising Him with all
I have.

Do you know that God wants us to experience His presence like that at all times? We are the ones who sometimes lose our way. (God has not nor will He ever lose anything.) I have noticed that in the presence of God, every care is extinct, all hurt is extinct, anger is extinct —they do not matter. All you think about is **love** —how much you can love and how much you want to please Him. That is the mind God always wants for us to have.

When we allow God to rule, everything else ceases. It must exit the room; and if we allow God to rule more often, it will never return. Think about it. When you love someone so much, you will do your best to honor him or her in every way. Well, that is the same way with God; He even honors us . . . He loves us so much.

Wow! He loved us so much that He sent our Savior, Jesus. The Father sent him to die, to die a cruel death, to be buried, and then to rise again. Hallelujah! No, we do not have to suffer torment by the devil's schemes. How many of us would put our children on death row for someone? No one that I can think of wants his or her child killed, or beaten or tortured, for that matter. God did that for us!

We need to remember *that* . . . we have taken that for granted. We must decide that we want to live a life that brings God joy. When we please God, we gain favor with Him and man. He already loves us but He wants a closer encounter with us, a daily encounter; so let us give Him that, okay! Give God that opportunity to show you real love, a love that you will never regret. Believe me, it feels so wonderful being loved by God and knowing it.

Closing

If you take a moment and examine where you are in life and if after that examination, you have discovered that there is no progress from where you last started, than there is a problem. Face it! Do something about it.

Keep in mind that with God we are always moving forward, so if progress has not occurred in your life, then it is time to get up. The prophet Elijah asked the widow woman whose sons were about to be sold into slavery, "What do you have?" God is asking us the same thing, "What do we have?" There is something inside of you so great that it is going to change generations to come, for the better. God created you to be the one to usher in that change. If you are unsure about *what* that is, then pray. Sometimes you have to fast and pray to get the answers you need.

Start with something that you love and if that does not seem to work, move on to something else; just keep on moving. I love music. I have always wanted to produce my own CD, and I did. It did not go so well because I was bad at producing; however, I was thankful that I did something I had never tried before. Another opportunity came to produce, which was a little better than the first. Although these CD's never hit the top 10, or the top 10,000, for that matter, the fact is I did what was in my heart and I used what I had —my ability to try, my love of writing, and my voice to sing. I have decided to leave the producing to the pros.

Hey, do you know that I even mustered up the courage to perform some of those songs at certain events? Those who heard them enjoyed every minute. That experience helped me to move past my fears and, through it all, I realized that my gifting was in writing. Yes, I was afraid of what people might say and yes, I was unsure . . . but if I were to get out of that familiar place of *nowhere* and move on to *better*, I had to act as if I had the courage and get going!

We all will have our own hurdles to get over; the key is to "get over" them. I found out that there were more people praising me for trying than were my own numerous thoughts taunting me with criticisms. Please, do not allow your mind to play tricks on you and stop your forward movement. Satan will try anything to stop you from moving forward; our mind is his playground. Just so that you know, there will always be critics; they are not going anywhere, so get use to it! Find out what it is you are afraid of and tackle it. Probably, it is *the one thing* that may cause you to prosper —so never allow the familiar and negative to hinder you.

Philippians 4:13 says, *"I can do all things through Christ who strengthens me."* So get up and make that change.

Terri

Terri Davis

Minister Terri Davis was born Teresa Ann Davis in Kansas City, Missouri, and was reared in Los Angeles, California. Terri began her career in the entertainment industry through music, with singing always being her first love. Her gift of writing started in Junior High School with poetry. Although writing first began as an outlet to express her feelings, Terri's poetry later developed and led to her writing songs…some for which she has been nominated and received awards.

Terri is an ordained minister and mother of three wonderful children, her nephew Tony, and has now has added the joy of son-in-laws-, and a beautiful grandchild named Evelyn Olivia.

This is the first of many inspirational books from Terri, who is truly "A Masterpiece in the Making."

CONTACT INFORMATION:

Terri Davis
Terrisings4God@gmail.com,
Terri_Davis1@yahoo.com

Made in the USA
Lexington, KY
28 October 2017